CUPCA

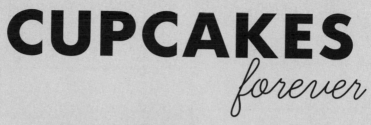

CUPCAKES
forever

DELICIOUS RECIPES FOR CUPCAKES
WITH LOVE FROM
LOLA'S

photography by
PETER CASSIDY

RYLAND PETERS & SMALL
LONDON • NEW YORK

Senior Designer Sonya Nathoo
Editor Alice Sambrook
Production Mai Ling Collyer
Art Director Leslie Harrington
Editorial Director Julia Charles
Publisher Cindy Richards

Food Stylist Bridget Sargeson
Prop Stylist Jenny Iggleden
Indexer Vanessa Bird
Illustrations Tracy Davy
US recipe testing and conversions
  Cathy Seward

Recipes in this book have been
developed by the Lola's Team of
Bakers, headed by Julia Head.
All baking tips and hints have
been carefully tested and selected
for this book by Julia Head.

First published in 2016 in the
United Kingdom
by Ryland Peters & Small
20–21 Jockey's Fields
London WC1R 4BW
and
341 East 116th Street
New York NY 10029
www.rylandpeters.com

The recipes in this book have
been previously published by
Ryland Peters & Small in
Lola's Forever, 2014.

Text © Lola's Kitchen Ltd.
Design and photographs
© Ryland Peters & Small 2014,
2016
Illustrations © Lola's Kitchen Ltd.

UK ISBN: 978-1-84975-767-6
US ISBN: 978-1-84975-766-9

10 9 8 7 6 5 4 3 2 1

Peter Cassidy is one of Europe's
most talented photographers. He
specializes in food and travel, and
his work often appears in magazines.
For Ryland Peters & Small, he has
photographed many books
including *Real Mexican Food*.

NOTES
• Both British (Metric) and
American (Imperial plus US cups)
are included in these recipes for
your convenience, however it is
important to work with one set of
measurements and not alternate
between the two within a recipe.
• All ingredients should be at room
temperature. Remove butter and
eggs from the refrigerator at least
30 minutes before baking.
• All spoon measurements are level,
unless otherwise specified.
• Ovens should be preheated to the
specified temperature. Recipes were
tested using a fan oven.
• All butter is unsalted, unless
otherwise specified.
• All eggs are free-range and large
(UK) or extra large (US), unless
otherwise specified. Recipes
containing raw or partially cooked
egg should not be served to the
very young, very old, anyone with
a compromised immune system or
pregnant women.
• When using the zest of citrus fruit,
try to find organic or unwaxed fruits
and wash well before using.
• The cases used in the book are
large. Muffin cases are
recommended.

CONTENTS

Lola's cupcakes

LOLA's is a business with a simple aim: to handcraft the most delicious cupcakes you have ever tasted, using only the finest fresh ingredients. LOLA's is run with passion and creativity by Asher Budwig, a fourth-generation baker who grew up watching his father Mario establish and run the enormously successful chain Millie's Cookies, which grew to over 100 stores in the UK. Asher's grandmother and great grandmother had also run a patisserie and café since the 1940s in Colombia, so with such a talented family of bakers, it was almost inevitable that he would bring success to LOLA's.

LOLA's is rapidly expanding, and Asher's passion for high standards and quality ingredients is reflected in the latest developments. In every new branch of LOLA's, quality remains key. The specialist bakers are highly trained and passionate about all things LOLA. Each individual cupcake is created with love and skill, so that every cupcake is sure to impress.

In this book, we want to let you in on some of our secrets, and share our favourite recipes that have made LOLA's so successful. All the best-loved cupcakes from LOLA's Classic Collection are included here, so you can create our famous Chocolate, Vanilla and Red Velvet cupcakes at home. With advice on achieving cake perfection and a guide to piping our signature swirl of frosting, you will be creating professional-looking morsels in no time.

Once you've mastered our Classic Collection, you will be ready to try your hand at a selection of our more unusual cupcakes. The Fruits and Flowers chapter offers delicious flavours like Passion Fruit, Rose and Pistachio and Elderflower cupcakes, as well as sugar free and lactose-free options, for those that want them. For a festive bake try the warming Ginger, Mince Pie or Maple Syrup cupcakes in the Sugar and Spice chapter. Kids will love the Cookies and Candies chapter, with fun creations such as the famous Rainbow Swirl cupcake, Blue Monster or Peanut Butter with a jam/jelly core. Divine Desserts showcases some of Lola's unique specialities – Raspberry Pavlova, Banoffee and Apple Crumble never fail to please. For grown-up palates, there is an array of cocktail-inspired delights, such as Cosmopolitan, Mojito and Pina Colada cupcakes, as well as a luxurious selection of decadently rich chocolate bakes in the After Dark chapter, such as Chocolate Chilli, Dark Chocolate Truffle and Chocolate Mint.

The enduring popularity of the cupcake knows no bounds, and they remain the most stylish of bakery treats. Their versatility is what makes them so successful, from simple classics that are perfect with afternoon tea or mid-morning coffee to extravagantly decorated creations that make delightful gifts at any time of year. With something at LOLA's for every occasion, what are you waiting for? Get your apron on and get baking!

Lola's tips for successful baking

BASIC EQUIPMENT

When baking, it is important to read through the recipe before you start and make sure you have the right equipment to hand. The last thing you need is to get halfway through a recipe and realize that you don't actually own a whisk! We have compiled a list of indispensable equipment for the home baker:

- Rubber spatula, useful for scraping down the bowl and incorporating ingredients into a batter.
- Sieve/strainer, important to remove any lumps from dry ingredients and seeds from fruit purées.
- Balloon whisk, useful for whipping cream or egg whites and for folding these into icings/frostings or batters.
- Scales, we prefer to use electronic scales as they are accurate at measuring liquids and solids. It is important that your ingredients are accurately measured.
- Measuring spoons and cups, crucial for adding exact measurements of ingredients.
- Mixing bowls, one large bowl and a few smaller heatproof bowls.
- Ice cream scoop, helpful when measuring out cupcake batter into muffin cases.
- An apple corer, not necessarily essential, but helpful when removing the 'core' from a cake to add a filling.
- Palette knife/metal spatula, can be used to spread icing/frosting onto cupcakes.

MIXERS

A stand mixer is every home cook's dream! We all covet the beautiful vintage mixers we see in the shops, however, there are cheaper models on the market that do just as good

a job and are very reasonably priced. A stand mixer cuts baking preparation time in half; however, with a little elbow grease, all our recipes can be made by hand. Most mixers will come with a paddle attachment, which is what we use when mixing our batters. Occasionally we will use the whisk attachment, mainly when beating eggs with sugar.

A hand-held electric whisk, the cousin of the stand mixer, is essential when whisking egg whites over heat for a marshmallow topping, and it can be used instead of a stand mixer when preparing our batters. A very useful piece of kit, it is relatively inexpensive to buy.

TINS AND PANS
We use muffin pans for all our cupcakes. They are slightly deeper than cupcake pans, and usually have 12 holes. Buy the best you can afford.

PIPING/PASTRY BAGS AND NOZZLES/TIPS
You can buy various sizes and shapes of nozzle/tip online. We often find that the nozzles/tips in baking kits are too small, but do experiment with different sizes to see what you like best. We recommend disposable piping/pastry bags, as they save you the task of washing them! For adding a 'core' to a cupcake, use a disposable piping bag with the end snipped off.

CUPCAKE CASES
We use muffin cases with dimensions of 5 cm/2 in. across the base and 3.8 cm/1 1/2 in. in height. For gluten-free cupcakes, we use foil cases rather than paper cases, as we find gluten-free flour bakes more evenly in these. Cases are available in supermarkets.

SPECIAL INGREDIENTS
When you decide to bake, you don't want to have to start shopping online for an obscure

ingredient, so we have tried to use ingredients and decorations that are available to the home cook. There are a few ingredients, however, we have not been able to locate within our local supermarkets and may require you to shop online or use a specialist baking outlet.

• Food colours, these vary from brand to brand. Most colourings for the domestic market are based on natural colourings, which, in our experience, do not give vibrant shades, so try online retailers for brighter colours.

• Sprinkles are now available in supermarkets in a wonderful array of shapes and sizes. For something specific, try online retailers.

MIXING THE BATTER

There are a few stages involved in preparing the perfect cupcake batter. We hope by providing you with a few tips, your baking experience will be simple and disaster-free!

The most important thing to do before you start is make sure that all your ingredients are at room temperature. We can't stress how important this is to your finished cake. Take butter and eggs out of the fridge 30 minutes before you start. If you are very short on time, you can bring cold eggs up to room temperature by placing them in a cup filled with tepid water. Cold butter can be cut into small pieces and placed in a very low microwave or saucepan to soften. Do not leave raw eggs at room temperature for longer than 30 minutes, and use immediately once brought up to room temperature. Preheat the oven to the temperature specified in the recipe.

The first stage with most of our recipes is to 'cream' the butter and sugar together. This really just means beating the softened butter with the sugar, incorporating a little air. If you have time, this can be done by hand with a wooden spoon, but it is much quicker and easier to do it in a stand mixer with the paddle attachment or in a mixing bowl with a hand-held electric whisk.

Next, we add the eggs, one at a time, mixing slowly until incorporated.

Do not worry if your mixture curdles after adding the eggs, this is very common and will normally be rectified once you have added the dry ingredients.

The dry ingredients are then added, but these must be sifted well first. At this stage, you can add any extras, such as nuts or chocolate.

FILLING THE CASES AND BAKING

The cake batter should be divided evenly between the muffin cases, to ensure that all your cupcakes are even sizes. We find the easiest way to transfer the batter to the cases is using an ice cream scoop. This ensures the same amount of batter goes in each case, and creates less mess than using teaspoons.

Once the cakes are in the oven, resist the urge to open the oven door until the baking time is complete. All these steps will ensure your finished product is perfect. Test to see if the cakes are cooked through by inserting a skewer into the centre of one cake – if it comes out clean, the cake is cooked.

ICINGS/FROSTINGS AND BUTTERCREAM

There are many different types of icing/frosting to try in our book. Every cupcake you create will look slightly different to the last one, but this is the best part about home-made cakes and hand-decorating them!

We have used a mixture of buttercreams and cream cheese icings in our finishes. The toppings have been paired with the cupcakes to create the best flavour combination possible. For example, the cream cheese recipe complements the Chocolate Guinness cupcake brilliantly, by cutting the rich cocoa base with a smooth, cool and not too sweet topping. We have used the buttercream on a lot of our classic range. It is easy to pipe and is simple to add colouring to. Finally, we use a delicious mascarpone icing on our tangy Mojito cupcake. This is really something special! We feel we have complemented our bases with the perfect icings/frostings, but feel free to mix and match toppings, if you like.

USING A PIPING/PASTRY BAG

At Lola's we prefer to use a disposable piping/pastry bag to pipe our finishes but know that not everyone likes to use a piping/pastry bag. Therefore, we wanted to give you a few hints and tips on how to pipe a 'Lola's swirl' on to your cupcakes. We will guide you through this process, from filling a piping/pastry bag to the finished result with some handy photographs to show you what you are aiming to achieve (see page 18).

To prepare your piping/pastry bag, slip the nozzle/tip into place in your piping bag. We like to use a large star nozzle/tip, but there are many shapes and sizes for you to choose from. You can create all sorts of different effects with various nozzles/tips.

Hold the bag just above the nozzle/tip and pull the remaining bag over your hand so that you have a smaller cone shape to fill. Using a rubber spatula, spoon your icing into the nose of the piping/pastry bag, nearest the nozzle/tip. Bring the excess bag back up over your hand and gently twist the top to push the icing down into the nozzle/tip. Work out any air bubbles that you can see by gently pushing the icing down the piping/pastry bag and twisting the top with your dominant hand.

Hold the piping/pastry bag at the top with your hand covering the twist and use your other hand to guide as you pipe. When piping any decoration, air can be your worst enemy, so be sure to remove all the air pockets before you start your creation.

WRITING ICING

For birthdays or special occasions, you can add text to your cupcakes. We find this is easiest on a flat-iced cake, using a small piping/pastry bag made from baking parchment. Cut a circle of baking parchment, make a cut from one edge to the centre, and then carefully curl the parchment into a cone shape. Hold the cone in the palm of your hand, carefully fill with melted chocolate or a dark tone of thinned down buttercream and fold the top edge over to seal the cone. Snip off the tip, and carefully squeeze to start the flow. Practise your detailing on a piece of parchment paper before you start decorating. Use the same technique as for icing a cake, being sure to use a short sharp lift when pulling away from your detailing. Practise makes perfect, you will soon get the hang of this skill!

THE LOLA'S SWIRL

At Lola's we have a signature swirl! If you want to recreate this at home, the step-by-step pictures below will help to guide you.

To pipe the Lola's swirl, start in the middle of your cupcake and gently squeeze the piping/pastry bag to get an initial star shape. Gently push the nozzle/tip into the icing and begin piping in an anticlockwise direction, covering the entire surface of the cake. Use the end of the nozzle/tip to guide you around the cake.

As you approach the end of your swirl push the nozzle into the icing and swiftly lift up and off the surface in a sideways motion to obtain a clean end to the swirl back in the centre of the cake. Don't worry if this is not perfect as you can use your sprinkles or other decorations to cover up any imperfections. Practise really does make perfect in this instance, and by the time you have iced the twelfth cupcake in your batch we are sure you will see an improvement in your technique!

OTHER PIPING EFFECTS

Various effects can be achieved with different nozzles/tips. Feel free to experiment – you don't have to stick to the style shown in the recipe. A small star nozzle/tip can be used to pipe lots of little stars on the top of a cake, or a large open star can create a less structured swirl. A plain round nozzle/tip can be used for an alternative swirl, too.

FLAT ICING

Take a small amount of buttercream and, using a palette knife/metal spatula, spread the buttercream over the surface of your cake. Using the palette knife/metal spatula, create the finish that you want. Little peaks of buttercream can look very nice, or some people prefer a smoother finish. Remove any excess until you are happy with the way it looks. This is much easier than piping and is a great option when time is short. If you want to add writing icing, you will need to finish the cake with a flat surface.

basic icing recipes

THESE ICING/FROSTING RECIPES ARE USED
THROUGHOUT THE BOOK IN VARIOUS FORMS.
THE CLASSIC VANILLA BUTTERCREAM GOES WELL
WITH ALMOST ANYTHING, RICH CHOCOLATE
BUTTERCREAM MAKES FOR A TRULY DECADENT
CUPCAKE AND A COOL CREAM CHEESE ICING
IS THE LIGHTER, LESS SWEET OPTION. MIX AND
MATCH TO CREATE YOUR IDEAL CUPCAKE
USING ANY OF THESE TRUSTED RECIPES.

basic vanilla buttercream

150 g/1¼ sticks butter
1 teaspoon vanilla bean paste
350 g/3 cups icing/
confectioners' sugar
3–4 tablespoons full-fat/whole
milk

To make the buttercream, place the butter into the bowl of a stand
mixer fitted with a paddle attachment (or use a hand-held electric
whisk), and beat until soft and fluffy. Add the vanilla bean paste and
mix again, until combined. Sift in half of the icing/confectioners' sugar
and, mixing at low speed, mix until incorporated. Add the second half
of the sugar, then beat slowly until all the sugar is incorporated. Add
the milk, a tablespoonful at a time, mixing at medium speed, until the
buttercream is light and fluffy. If the icing is too stiff, add a little
more milk.

basic chocolate buttercream

150 g/1 1/4 sticks butter
40 g/1/3 cup unsweetened
  cocoa powder
300 g/2 1/2 cups icing/
  confectioners' sugar
60–75 ml/4–5 tablespoons full-
  fat/whole milk

For the buttercream, place the butter into the bowl of a stand mixer fitted with a paddle attachment (or use a hand-held electric whisk), and beat the mixture at medium to high speed, until smooth and soft. In another bowl, sift the cocoa powder and icing/confectioners' sugar together. Turn the mixer to low speed and add the sifted cocoa powder and sugar, a little at a time, to the butter. When it is incorporated, turn the mixer to medium speed and add the milk, a tablespoonful at a time, until the buttercream is smooth. Beat on high speed, until light and fluffy. If the buttercream is too stiff, add a little more milk to soften.

basic cream cheese icing

60 g/1/2 stick butter
1 teaspoon vanilla bean paste
200 g/1 3/4 cups icing/
  confectioners' sugar
400 g/14 oz. full-fat cream
  cheese

To make the cream cheese icing, place the butter into the bowl of a stand mixer fitted with a paddle attachment (or use a hand-held electric whisk), and beat until smooth and soft. Add the vanilla bean paste and sift in the icing/confectioners' sugar. Add the cream cheese and beat at medium to high speed for about 30 seconds, until smooth and glossy. Do not over-mix.

CLASSIC COLLECTION

VANILLA CUPCAKE

EGG-FREE VANILLA CUPCAKE

CHOCOLATE CUPCAKE

ROCKY ROAD CUPCAKE

RED VELVET CUPCAKE

GLUTEN-FREE RED VELVET CUPCAKE

CARROT CUPCAKE

SALTED TOFFEE POPCORN CUPCAKE

BANANA CUPCAKE

WHITE CHOCOLATE CUPCAKE

COFFEE AND WALNUT CUPCAKE

vanilla cupcake

HERE WE USE A SIMPLE BUTTERCREAM FLECKED WITH VANILLA BEAN PASTE TO
COMPLEMENT THE BUTTERY SPONGE. LET YOUR CREATIVITY RUN RIOT DECORATING!

200 g self-raising flour/
   1 1/2 cups cake flour mixed
   with 3 teaspoons baking
   powder
1 teaspoon baking powder
175 g/1 1/2 sticks butter
250 g/1 1/4 cups caster/
   granulated sugar
1 1/2 teaspoons vanilla bean
   paste
3 eggs
175 ml/3/4 cup sour cream

BUTTERCREAM
1 quantity Basic Vanilla
   Buttercream (see page 20)

TO DECORATE
sugar flowers and sprinkles
   of your choice

muffin pan lined with 12 muffin
   cases

piping/pastry bag fitted with
   a large star nozzle/tip

MAKES 12

Preheat the oven to 180°C (350°F) Gas 4.

Sift the flour and baking powder into a bowl and set aside.

Place the butter and sugar into the bowl of a stand mixer fitted
with a paddle attachment (or use a hand-held electric whisk), and beat
the mixture at medium to high speed for 1–2 minutes, until light and
fluffy. Occasionally stop to scrape down the sides of the bowl with a
rubber spatula to make sure that all the butter and sugar is incorporated.

Add the vanilla bean paste and mix. Then, at low speed, add the eggs,
one at a time, until fully incorporated.

Slowly add the sifted dry ingredients, and mix at low speed until
combined. Scrape down the sides of the bowl with a rubber spatula, and
briefly beat at high speed until the mixture is smooth. Add the sour
cream and mix until incorporated. Do not over-mix.

Using an ice cream scoop, divide the mixture between the muffin
cases, filling to almost two-thirds full. Bake in the preheated oven for
20–25 minutes, until well risen and a skewer inserted into the cakes
comes out clean. Transfer to a wire rack to cool completely.

Prepare the Basic Vanilla Buttercream following the instructions
on page 20.

Spoon the buttercream into the piping/pastry bag, and pipe a swirl
of buttercream onto each cupcake. Alternatively, spread the buttercream
onto each cake using a palette knife or metal spatula. Decorate with
sugar flowers and sprinkles.

egg-free vanilla cupcake

45 g/¹/₃ cup cornflour/
  cornstarch
180 g/1¹/₃ cups plain/
  all-purpose flour
1¹/₄ teaspoons baking powder
¹/₄ teaspoon bicarbonate
  of soda/baking soda
160 g/1¹/₂ sticks butter, melted
315 g/1 cup natural/plain
  yogurt
125 g/²/₃ cup caster/
  granulated sugar
1¹/₂ teaspoons vanilla bean
  paste

BUTTERCREAM
1 quantity Basic Vanilla
  Buttercream (see page 20)

TO DECORATE
36 fresh raspberries
raspberry coulis or
  sieved/strained raspberry
  jam/jelly

muffin pan lined with
  12 muffin cases

piping/pastry bag fitted with
  a small star nozzle/tip

MAKES 12

WE REALIZE THAT SOME OF OUR CUSTOMERS HAVE INTOLERANCES TO CERTAIN FOODS, SO THIS EGG-FREE CUPCAKE IS FOR THOSE WHO FIND IT HARD TO ENJOY OUR USUAL CUPCAKES. WE THINK IT IS JUST AS DELICIOUS AND URGE YOU TO EXPERIMENT WITH DIFFERENT TOPPINGS.

Preheat the oven to 180°C (350°F) Gas 4.

Sift the cornflour/cornstarch, plain/all-purpose flour, baking powder and bicarbonate of soda/baking soda into a large bowl and set aside.

In a separate bowl, whisk the melted butter with the yogurt, sugar and vanilla bean paste, until the sugar is dissolved. It is easy to do this with a large balloon whisk – it will take 1–2 minutes.

Carefully add the sifted dry ingredients into the wet ingredients, using the whisk to combine.

Using an ice cream scoop, divide the mixture between the muffin cases, filling to almost two-thirds full. Bake in the preheated oven for 25–28 minutes, until well risen and a skewer inserted into the cakes comes out clean. Transfer to a wire rack to cool completely.

Prepare the Basic Vanilla Buttercream following the instructions on page 20.

Spoon the buttercream into the piping/pastry bag and pipe stars around the top of each cupcake. Alternatively, spread the buttercream onto each cupcake using a palette knife or metal spatula. Decorate each cupcake with 3 fresh raspberries and a drizzle of coulis.

At Lola's, we also use a chocolate buttercream to decorate this egg-free cupcake, so feel free to experiment with other icings once you have mastered the egg-free cupcake base!

chocolate cupcake

A LIGHT AND FLUFFY, MOIST CHOCOLATE CAKE TOPPED WITH OUR
DELICIOUS CHOCOLATE BUTTERCREAM AND DECORATED IN A FUN STYLE.

3 eggs
220 g/1 cup caster/
   granulated sugar
150 ml/²/₃ cup sunflower oil
80 ml/¹/₃ cup full-fat/whole
   milk
150 g self-raising flour/
   1 cup cake flour mixed
   with 2 teaspoons baking
   powder, sifted
45 g/generous ¹/₃ cup
   unsweetened cocoa
   powder

BUTTERCREAM
1 quantity Basic Chocolate
   Buttercream (see page 21)

TO DECORATE
chocolate stars and
   sprinkles of your choice

muffin pan lined with
   12 muffin cases

piping/pastry bag fitted with
   a large star nozzle/tip

MAKES 12

Preheat the oven to 180°C (350°F) Gas 1.

Place the eggs and sugar into the bowl of a stand mixer fitted with
a whisk attachment (or use a hand-held electric whisk), and beat the
mixture at medium to high speed for 1–2 minutes, until light and fluffy.

If using a stand mixer, switch to the paddle attachment. Combine the
oil and milk, then slowly add to the egg mixture, and mix until just
combined. Sift the flour and cocoa powder together into a separate
bowl, and add to the batter, a little at a time, beating until incorporated.
Scrape down the sides of the bowl with a rubber spatula, and briefly beat
at high speed until the mixture is smooth. Do not over-mix.

Using an ice cream scoop, divide the mixture between the muffin
cases, filling to almost two-thirds full. Bake in the preheated oven for
20–25 minutes, until well risen and a skewer inserted into the cakes
comes out clean. Transfer to a wire rack to cool completely.

Prepare the Basic Chocolate Buttercream following the instructions
on page 21.

To decorate, spoon the buttercream into the piping/pastry bag,
and pipe a swirl onto the tops of the cupcakes. Alternatively, spread
the buttercream onto each cake using a palette knife or metal spatula.
Decorate each cupcake with a chocolate star and some sprinkles.

*This is a great basic recipe
with which you can experiment.*

rocky road cupcake

THE ROCKY ROAD CUPCAKE HAS IT ALL! SQUIDGY MARSHMALLOWS, SOUR CHERRIES, CRUNCHY BISCUIT PIECES, TOASTED ALMONDS AND SILKY BUTTERCREAM.

ROCKY ROAD
50 g/3¹/₂ tablespoons butter
125 g/³/₄ cup chopped dark/bittersweet chocolate
1 tablespoon golden/light corn syrup
75 g/³/₄ cup crumbled digestive biscuits/graham crackers
40 g/³/₄ cup mini marshmallows
40 g/¹/₄ cup dried sour cherries, chopped
40 g/¹/₃ cup toasted flaked/sliced almonds

18-cm/7-in square cake pan, greased and lined with baking parchment

CHOCOLATE CAKE
1 egg
75 g/6 tablespoons caster/granulated sugar
50 ml/¹/₄ cup sunflower oil
2 tablespoons full-fat/whole milk
1 tablespoon unsweetened cocoa powder

To make the rocky road, place the butter, chocolate and syrup in a saucepan. Heat gently until melted. Set aside to cool slightly. Place the biscuit/cracker crumbs, marshmallows, cherries and almonds in a large bowl, and pour over the chocolate mixture. Mix with a wooden spoon, then pour into the prepared pan. Chill in the refrigerator for at least an hour, until set.

Preheat the oven to 180°C (350°F) Gas 4.

To make the chocolate cake mixture, place the egg and sugar into the bowl of a stand mixer fitted with a whisk attachment (or use a hand-held electric whisk), and beat the mixture at medium to high speed for 1–2 minutes, until light and fluffy.

If using a stand mixer, switch to the paddle attachment. Combine the oil and milk, then slowly add to the egg mixture, and mix just until combined. Sift the cocoa powder and flour into a separate bowl, and add to the batter, a little at a time, beating until incorporated. Scrape down the sides of the bowl with a rubber spatula, and briefly beat at high speed until the mixture is smooth. Do not over-mix. Add the marshmallows and cherries and fold in, using the rubber spatula.

For the vanilla cake, place the butter and sugar into the bowl of a stand mixer fitted with a paddle attachment (or use a hand-held electric whisk), and beat for 30 seconds, until light and fluffy. Add the eggs and vanilla bean paste, and mix at low speed until combined. Sift the flour and baking powder into a separate bowl, and add to the batter, a little at a time, beating at low speed until incorporated. Add the sour cream and mix until smooth. Do not over-mix.

50 g self-raising flour/
  $1/3$ cup cake flour mixed
  with $1/2$ teaspoon baking
  powder
30 g/$1/2$ cup chopped
  marshmallows
40 g/$1/3$ cup dried sour
  cherries

VANILLA CAKE
90 g/$3/4$ stick butter
125 g/$2/3$ cup caster/
  granulated sugar
2 eggs
$1/2$ teaspoon vanilla bean
  paste

Divide the vanilla batter evenly between the muffin cases. Do the same with the chocolate batter, placing it on top of the vanilla mixture already in the cases. Using the tip of a knife, swirl the two batters together to blend them slightly. Bake in the preheated oven for 20–23 minutes, until well risen and a skewer inserted into the cakes comes out clean. Transfer to a wire rack to cool completely.

For the buttercream, place the butter into the bowl of a stand mixer fitted with a paddle attachment (or use a hand-held electric whisk), and beat until soft and fluffy. Divide the butter evenly between two bowls. Sift half the icing/confectioners' sugar into one bowl, and slowly mix until combined. Add the vanilla bean paste and enough of the milk to achieve a consistency suitable for piping. Sift the rest of the icing/confectioners'

100 g self-raising flour/
   ¾ cup cake flour mixed
   with 2 teaspoons baking
   powder
½ teaspoon baking powder
85 ml/⅓ cup sour cream

BUTTERCREAM
200 g/2 sticks minus 2
   tablespoons butter
400 g/3½ cups icing/
   confectioners' sugar
½ teaspoon vanilla bean
   paste
6–10 teaspoons full-fat/whole
   milk
2 tablespoons unsweetened
   cocoa powder

*muffin pan lined with
   12 muffin cases*

*piping/pastry bag fitted with
   a large star nozzle/tip*

MAKES 12

sugar into the other bowl along with the cocoa powder, and slowly mix until combined. Add enough of the milk to achieve a suitable piping consistency.

Spoon the vanilla buttercream down one side of the piping/pastry bag and spoon the chocolate buttercream down the other side. This will create a marbled effect when piped.

Turn the rocky road out onto a chopping board. Using a sharp knife, slice it into at least 24 small pieces.

Pipe the buttercream onto each cake in a swirl. Some cakes will have more chocolate buttercream and others will have more vanilla, which makes each cupcake individual. Top each cupcake with a couple of pieces of rocky road.

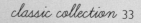

red velvet cupcake

WE ADD MELTED CHOCOLATE AND GROUND ALMONDS TO OUR RED VELVET CUPCAKE
TO KEEP IT MOIST AND MOREISH, AND TOP IT OFF WITH A CREAM CHEESE ICING.

110 g/1 stick butter
160 g/¾ cup caster/
  granulated sugar
1 teaspoon vanilla bean paste
½ teaspoon red food
  colouring paste
1 egg
3 tablespoons sunflower oil
¾ tablespoon white wine
  vinegar or freshly squeezed
  lemon juice
35 g/1¼ oz. dark/bittersweet
  chocolate, melted
190 g/1⅓ cups plain/
  all-purpose flour
½ teaspoon baking powder
½ teaspoon bicarbonate of
  soda/baking soda
¾ tablespoon unsweetened
  cocoa powder
70 ml/scant ⅓ cup single/light
  cream
70 ml/scant ⅓ cup full-fat/
  whole milk
35 g/¼ cup ground almonds

CREAM CHEESE ICING
1 quantity Basic Cream
  Cheese Icing (see page 21)

TO DECORATE
red velvet cake crumbs

*muffin pan lined with
  12 muffin cases*

*piping/pastry bag fitted with
  a large star nozzle/tip*

MAKES 12

Preheat the oven to 180°C (350°F) Gas 4.

Place the butter, sugar and vanilla bean paste into the bowl of a stand mixer fitted with a paddle attachment (or use a hand-held electric whisk), and beat the mixture at medium to high speed for 1–2 minutes, until light and fluffy. Occasionally stop to scrape down the sides of the bowl with a rubber spatula to make sure that all the butter and sugar is incorporated.

Add the food colouring paste and the egg, and beat slowly until combined. Beat in the oil and vinegar or lemon juice, followed by the melted chocolate.

Sift the flour, baking powder, bicarbonate of soda/baking soda and unsweetened cocoa powder together into a separate bowl. Add the dry ingredients to the batter, a little at a time, alternating with the cream and milk until you have a soft batter and all the dry ingredients have been incorporated. Finally, add the ground almonds and mix until smooth and a uniform colour. Scrape down the sides of the bowl with a rubber spatula, and briefly beat at high speed until the mixture is smooth. Do not over-mix.

Using an ice cream scoop, divide the mixture between the muffin cases, filling to almost two-thirds full. Bake in the preheated oven for 18–22 minutes, or until risen and a skewer inserted into the cakes comes out clean. Transfer to a wire rack to cool completely.

Prepare the Basic Cream Cheese Icing following the instructions on page 21.

Spoon the icing into the piping/pastry bag, and pipe a swirl onto each cake. Alternatively, spread the cream cheese icing onto each cupcake using a palette knife or metal spatula. Decorate with red velvet cake crumbs.

THIS GLUTEN-FREE VERSION ALLOWS COELIACS/CELIACS
TO ENJOY THIS FAVOURITE, LOSING NONE OF THE FLAVOUR.

gluten-free red velvet cupcake

110 g/1 stick butter
160 g/³/4 cup caster/granulated sugar
1 teaspoon vanilla bean paste
³/4 teaspoon red food colouring paste
1 egg
3 tablespoons sunflower oil
³/4 tablespoon white wine vinegar or freshly squeezed lemon juice
35 g/1¹/4 oz. dark/bittersweet chocolate, melted
190 g/1¹/3 cups gluten-free plain/all-purpose flour
¹/2 teaspoon gluten-free baking powder
¹/2 teaspoon bicarbonate of soda/baking soda
³/4 tablespoon unsweetened cocoa powder
70 ml/scant ¹/3 cup single/light cream
70 ml/scant ¹/3 cup full-fat/whole milk
35 g/¹/4 cup ground almonds

CREAM CHEESE ICING
1 quantity Basic Cream Cheese Icing (see page 21)

TO DECORATE
red velvet cake crumbs

muffin pan lined with 12 muffin cases

piping/pastry bag fitted with a large star nozzle/tip

MAKES 12

Preheat the oven to 180°C (350°F) Gas 4.

Place the butter, sugar and vanilla bean paste into the bowl of a stand mixer fitted with a paddle attachment (or use a hand-held electric whisk), and beat the mixture at medium to high speed for 1–2 minutes, until light and fluffy. Occasionally stop to scrape down the sides of the bowl with a rubber spatula to make sure that all the butter and sugar is incorporated.

Add the food colouring paste and the egg, and beat slowly until combined. Beat in the oil and vinegar or lemon juice, followed by the melted chocolate.

Sift the gluten-free flour, baking powder, bicarbonate of soda/baking soda and unsweetened cocoa powder together into a separate bowl. Add the dry ingredients to the batter, a little at a time, alternating with the cream and milk until you have a soft batter and all the dry ingredients have been incorporated. Finally, add the ground almonds and mix until smooth and a uniform colour. Scrape down the sides of the bowl with a rubber spatula, and briefly beat at high speed until the mixture is smooth. Do not over-mix.

Using an ice cream scoop, divide the mixture between the muffin cases, filling to almost two-thirds full. Bake in the preheated oven for 18–22 minutes, or until risen and a skewer inserted into the cakes comes out clean. Transfer to a wire rack to cool completely.

Prepare the Basic Cream Cheese Icing following the instructions on page 21.

Spoon the icing into the piping/pastry bag, and pipe a swirl onto each cake. Alternatively, spread the cream cheese icing onto each cupcake using a palette knife or metal spatula. Decorate with red velvet cake crumbs.

carrot cupcake

200 g/1 1/4 cups caster/
  granulated sugar
2 eggs
110 ml/1/3 cup sunflower oil
1 teaspoon vanilla bean paste
175 g/1 1/3 cups plain/
  all-purpose flour
1 teaspoon ground cinnamon
1 teaspoon baking powder
1/2 teaspoon bicarbonate
  of soda/baking soda
200 g/2 cups coarsely
  grated/shredded carrot
40 g/1/8 cup crushed pineapple
  (or finely chopped
  pineapple chunks)
30 g/1/4 cup finely chopped
  walnuts

CREAM CHEESE ICING
1 quantity Basic Cream
  Cheese Icing (see page 21)

TO DECORATE
finely chopped walnuts

*muffin pan lined with
  12 muffin cases*

*piping/pastry bag fitted with
  a small star nozzle/tip*

MAKES 12

LOLA'S DELECTABLE CARROT CUPCAKE HAS A SECRET
INGREDIENT – PINEAPPLE, WHICH HELPS KEEP IT MOIST AND
FRUITY. FINISHED WITH OUR DELICIOUS CREAM CHEESE ICING,
IT IS PERFECT WITH A MID-MORNING CUP OF TEA.

Preheat the oven to 180°C (350°F) Gas 4.

Place the sugar and eggs into the bowl of a stand mixer fitted with
a whisk attachment (or use a hand-held electric whisk), and beat the
mixture at medium to high speed for 1–2 minutes, until light and fluffy.

If using a stand mixer, switch to the paddle attachment. Gradually add
the oil and vanilla bean paste, mixing at low speed until just combined.

Sift the flour, cinnamon, baking powder and bicarbonate of soda/baking
soda into a separate bowl, then add to the batter, a little at a time,
beating until incorporated. Scrape down the sides of the bowl with
a rubber spatula, then add the grated carrot, crushed pineapple and
chopped walnuts. Mix until blended. Do not over-mix.

Using an ice cream scoop, divide the mixture between the muffin
cases, filling to almost two-thirds full. Bake in the preheated oven for
20–25 minutes, until well risen and a skewer inserted into the cakes
comes out clean. Transfer to a wire rack to cool completely.

Prepare the Basic Cream Cheese Icing following the instructions
on page 21.

Spoon the cream cheese icing into the piping/pastry bag and pipe stars
of icing onto the top of each cupcake. Alternatively, spread the icing onto
each cupcake using a palette knife or metal spatula. Decorate each
cupcake with a sprinkling of finely chopped walnuts.

salted toffee popcorn cupcake

YOU CAN'T BEAT SALTED CARAMEL! THIS DELICIOUS CUPCAKE HIDES A CARAMEL
CORE AND IS TOPPED WITH SALTED CARAMEL ICING AND STICKY TOFFEE POPCORN.

200 g self-raising flour/1 1/2
  cups cake flour mixed with
  1 teaspoon baking powder
1 teaspoon baking powder
175 g/1 1/2 sticks butter
250 g/1 cup caster/
  granulated sugar
1 1/2 teaspoons vanilla bean
  paste
3 eggs
175 ml/3/4 cup sour cream

BUTTERCREAM
125 g/1 1/8 sticks butter
1 teaspoon vanilla bean paste
250 g/2 cups icing/
  confectioners' sugar
1/4 teaspoon sea salt flakes (or
  to taste)
150 g/1/2 cup store-bought
  caramel
1 tablespoon full-fat/
  whole milk (optional)

CARAMEL CORE
125 g/1/3 cup store-bought
  caramel

TO DECORATE
36 pieces toffee popcorn

*muffin pan lined with
  12 muffin cases*

*piping/pastry bag fitted with
  a large star nozzle/tip*

MAKES 12

Preheat the oven to 180°C (350°F) Gas 4.

Sift the flour and baking powder into a bowl and set aside.

Place the butter and sugar into the bowl of a stand mixer fitted with a paddle attachment (or use a hand-held electric whisk), and beat the mixture at medium to high speed for 1–2 minutes, until light and fluffy. Occasionally stop to scrape down the sides of the bowl with a rubber spatula to make sure that all the butter and sugar is incorporated.

Add the vanilla bean paste and mix. Mixing at low speed, add the eggs, one at a time, beating until incorporated.

Slowly add the sifted dry ingredients, and mix at low speed until combined. Scrape down the sides of the bowl with a rubber spatula, and briefly beat at high speed until the mixture is smooth. Add the sour cream and mix until incorporated. Do not over-mix.

Using an ice cream scoop, divide the mixture between the muffin cases, filling to almost two-thirds full. Bake in the preheated oven for 20–25 minutes, until well risen and a skewer inserted into the cakes comes out clean. Transfer to a wire rack to cool completely.

To make the buttercream, place the butter into the bowl of a stand mixer fitted with a paddle attachment (or use a hand-held electric whisk), and beat until soft and fluffy. Add the vanilla bean paste and mix until combined. Sift in half of the icing/confectioners' sugar and, with the mixer on low speed, mix until incorporated. Add the second half of the sugar and the sea salt, then beat until all the sugar is incorporated. Add the caramel, a tablespoon at a time, mixing at medium speed, until the buttercream is light and fluffy. If it is too stiff, add the milk.

To make the caramel core, use a sharp knife or apple corer to remove a small section from the centre of each cupcake. Using a teaspoon (or disposable piping/pastry bag), fill the holes almost to the top with caramel.

Spoon the buttercream into the piping/pastry bag and pipe a star of buttercream onto the top of each cupcake. Alternatively, spread the buttercream onto the top of each cake using a palette knife or metal spatula. Arrange two or three pieces of toffee popcorn on the top of each cupcake to decorate.

classic collection 41

banana cupcake

AT LOLA'S WE ARE HUGE BANANA FANS AND WHAT A GREAT WAY TO GET OUR DAILY DOSE. A MOIST, LIGHT BANANA-SCENTED SPONGE TOPPED OFF WITH OUR CLASSIC COOL CREAM CHEESE ICING. A FIRM FAVOURITE WITH THE LOLA'S TEAM.

2 eggs
180 g/1 cup minus 1½ tablespoons caster/granulated sugar
100 ml/scant ½ cup sunflower oil
1 teaspoon vanilla bean paste
2 large bananas, mashed
185 g/1¼ cups plain/all-purpose flour
1 teaspoon bicarbonate of soda/baking soda
1 teaspoon ground cinnamon

CREAM CHEESE ICING
1 quantity Basic Cream Cheese Icing (see page 21)

TO DECORATE
1 banana, sliced into 12 or dried banana chips
ground cinnamon

muffin pan lined with 12 muffin cases

piping/pastry bag fitted with a large star nozzle/tip

MAKES 12

Preheat the oven to 180°C (350°F) Gas 4.

Place the eggs and sugar into the bowl of a stand mixer fitted with a whisk attachment (or use a hand-held electric whisk), and beat the mixture at medium to high speed for 1–2 minutes, until light and fluffy.

If using a stand mixer, switch to the paddle attachment. Add the oil and vanilla bean paste, and mix until just combined. Add the mashed bananas and mix. Sift the flour, bicarbonate of soda/baking soda and ground cinnamon into a separate bowl, then add to the batter, a little at a time, beating until incorporated. Scrape down the sides of the bowl with a rubber spatula, and briefly beat at high speed until the mixture is smooth. Do not over-mix.

Using an ice cream scoop, divide the mixture between the muffin cases, filling to almost two-thirds full.

Bake in the preheated oven for 20–25 minutes, until well risen and a skewer inserted into the cakes comes out clean. Transfer to a wire rack to cool completely.

Prepare the Basic Cream Cheese Icing following the instructions on page 21.

Spoon the cream cheese icing into the piping/pastry bag and pipe a swirl onto each cupcake. Alternatively, spread the icing onto each cupcake using a palette knife or metal spatula. Finish with a slice of banana or dried banana chip. Sprinkle with a little cinnamon.

white chocolate cupcake

THIS CUPCAKE IS A REAL TREAT. THERE IS SOMETHING VERY COMFORTING ABOUT WHITE CHOCOLATE WITH ITS HEADY VANILLA SCENT. THIS CUPCAKE DELIVERS AN EXTRA COCOA HIT IN THE FORM OF OUR BLACK BOTTOM BASE. TO CUT THE RICHNESS OF THE WHITE CHOCOLATE WE HAVE INCLUDED A FRESH BERRY CORE AND TOPPING.

100 g/³/₄ cup plain/
   all-purpose flour
65 g/²/₃ cup unsweetened
   cocoa powder
1 teaspoon baking powder
3 eggs
250 g/1¹/₄ cups caster/
   granulated sugar
2 tablespoons full-fat/whole
   milk
175 g/1¹/₂ sticks butter, melted

FRESH BERRY CORE
100 g/3¹/₂ oz. strawberries
125 g/4¹/₂ oz. raspberries
2 tablespoons raspberry
   jam/jelly

Preheat the oven to 180°C (350°F) Gas 4.

Sift the flour, cocoa powder and baking powder into a large bowl, and set aside.

Place the eggs and sugar into the bowl of a stand mixer fitted with a whisk attachment (or use a hand-held electric whisk), and beat the mixture at medium to high speed for 1–2 minutes, until light and fluffy.

If using a stand mixer, switch to the paddle attachment. Add the sifted dry ingredients to the batter along with the milk, mixing at low speed to combine. Add the melted butter and beat until blended. Do not over-mix.

Using an ice cream scoop, divide the mixture between the muffin cases, filling to almost two-thirds full. Bake in the preheated oven for 20–25 minutes, until well risen and a skewer inserted into the cakes comes out clean. Transfer to a wire rack to cool completely.

To make the fresh berry core, place the strawberries, raspberries and jam/jelly into a blender or food processor, and blend until almost smooth – it is quite nice to have a little texture to the purée, but this is entirely up to you. You can sieve/strain it to remove any seeds, if you like. Alternatively, mash with a fork.

BUTTERCREAM

150 g/1 1/4 sticks butter
1/2 teaspoon vanilla bean paste
350 g/3 cups icing/
    confectioners' sugar
50 g/1 3/4 oz. white chocolate,
    melted
2–3 tablespoons full-fat/
    whole milk

TO DECORATE

12 strawberries, halved
12 raspberries

muffin pan lined with
    12 muffin cases

piping/pastry bag fitted with
    a large star nozzle/tip

MAKES 12

To make the buttercream, place the butter into the bowl of a stand mixer fitted with a paddle attachment (or use a hand-held electric whisk), and beat until soft and fluffy. Add the vanilla bean paste and mix again, until combined. Sift in half of the icing/confectioners' sugar and, mixing at low speed, mix until incorporated. Add the second half of the sugar, then beat slowly, until all the sugar has been incorporated. Add the melted white chocolate and the milk, and beat at medium speed until light and fluffy. If the buttercream is stiff, add a little more milk.

To assemble the cupcakes, use a sharp knife or apple corer to remove a small section from the centre of each cupcake. Using a teaspoon (or disposable piping/pastry bag), fill the holes almost to the top with the fresh berry filling.

Spoon the buttercream into the piping/pastry bag and pipe a swirl or rose onto each cupcake. Alternatively, spread the buttercream onto each cake using a palette knife or metal spatula. Arrange two strawberry halves and a fresh raspberry on the top of each cupcake to decorate.

Using a good-quality white chocolate is important, try different brands before incorporating in your delicious bakes and treats so you know what you're working with.

coffee and walnut cupcake

A REAL TEATIME CLASSIC, TAKEN UP A NOTCH BY THE ADDITION OF A DELICIOUS DARK CHOCOLATE GANACHE CENTRE. WE LIKE TO USE INSTANT ESPRESSO POWDER MADE TO DOUBLE STRENGTH, BUT YOU CAN USE FRESHLY BREWED ESPRESSO COFFEE INSTEAD IF YOU PREFER. WE HOPE YOU ENJOY OUR TAKE ON THIS CLASSIC.

175 g/1½ sticks butter
175 g/¾ cup plus 2 tablespoons soft light brown sugar
3 eggs
175 g self-raising flour/ 1⅓ cups cake flour mixed with 2 teaspoons baking powder
3 tablespoons extra-strong espresso, cooled
50 g/½ cup chopped walnuts

GANACHE CORE
120 ml/½ cup double/ heavy cream
80 g/½ cup chopped dark/bittersweet chocolate (up to 60% cocoa solids)

Preheat the oven to 180°C (350°F) Gas 4.

Place the butter and sugar into the bowl of a stand mixer fitted with a paddle attachment (or use a hand-held electric whisk), and beat the mixture at medium to high speed for 1–2 minutes, until light and fluffy. Occasionally stop to scrape down the sides of the bowl with a rubber spatula to make sure that all the butter and sugar is incorporated.

On low speed, add the eggs, one at a time, beating until all the egg is fully incorporated into the mixture. Sift the flour into a separate bowl, then slowly add the sifted flour into the batter along with the cooled espresso, beating at low speed, until combined. Scrape down the sides of the bowl with a rubber spatula, and briefly beat at high speed until the mixture is smooth. Do not over-mix. Add the walnuts and mix.

BUTTERCREAM
150 g/1¼ sticks butter
350 g/3 cups icing/
    confectioners' sugar
3 tablespoons extra-strong
    espresso, cooled

TO DECORATE
chopped walnuts

*muffin pan lined with
    12 muffin cases*

*piping/pastry bag fitted with
    a large star nozzle/tip*

MAKES 12

Using an ice cream scoop, divide the mixture between the muffin cases, filling to almost two-thirds full. Bake in the preheated oven for 18–23 minutes, until well risen and a skewer inserted into the cakes comes out clean. Transfer to a wire rack to cool completely.

To make the ganache core, place the double/heavy cream in a small saucepan and heat until almost at boiling point. Place the chopped chocolate in a heatproof bowl. Pour the hot cream over the chopped chocolate and stir to combine. The mixture will be smooth and glossy. Allow to cool, then cover and place in the refrigerator to set.

To make the buttercream, place the butter into the bowl of a stand mixer fitted with a paddle attachment (or use a hand-held electric whisk), and beat until soft and fluffy. Sift in half of the icing/confectioners' sugar and slowly mix until incorporated. Add the second half of the sugar, then beat, slowly, until all the sugar has been incorporated. Add the cooled espresso, a tablespoonful at a time, mixing at a medium speed, until the buttercream is light and fluffy.

To assemble the cupcakes, use a sharp knife or apple corer to remove a small section from the centre of each cooled cupcake. Using a teaspoon (or disposable piping/pastry bag), fill the holes almost to the top with ganache.

Spoon the buttercream into the piping/pastry bag, and pipe a swirl onto the top of each cupcake. Alternatively, spread the buttercream onto each cake using a palette knife or metal spatula. Finish with a sprinkling of chopped walnuts to decorate.

FRUITS AND FLOWERS

LEMON POPPY SEED CUPCAKE

BLUEBERRY CUPCAKE

SUGAR-FREE BLUEBERRY CUPCAKE

MANGO CUPCAKE

PASSION FRUIT CUPCAKE

LACTOSE-FREE STRAWBERRY CUPCAKE

ROSE AND PISTACHIO CUPCAKE

ELDERFLOWER CUPCAKE

lemon poppy seed cupcake

HERE AT LOLA'S WE ARE BIG CITRUS FANS, AND THIS LEMON CUPCAKE DOES NOT DISAPPOINT. A POPPY SEED SPONGE IS SOAKED IN LEMON SYRUP AND TOPPED WITH A LIGHT BUTTERCREAM.

225 g self-raising flour/
  1¾ cups cake flour mixed
  with 4 teaspoons baking
  powder
½ teaspoon baking powder
175 g/¾ cup plus 2
  tablespoons caster/
  granulated sugar
grated zest from 2 lemons
3 eggs
50 g/¼ cup lemon curd
75 g/⅓ cup sour cream
175 g/1½ sticks butter, melted
2 tablespoons poppy seeds

SYRUP
freshly squeezed juice
  of 2 lemons
60 g/¼ cup sugar

BUTTERCREAM
200 g/1¾ sticks butter
400 g/scant 3½ cups icing/
  confectioners' sugar
75 g/⅓ cup lemon curd
1–2 tablespoons full-fat/
  whole milk

TO DECORATE
lemon zest, lemon curd and
  poppy seeds

muffin pan lined with
  12 muffin cases

piping/pastry bag fitted with
  a large star nozzle/tip

MAKES 12

Preheat the oven to 180°C (350°F) Gas 4.

Sift the flour and baking powder into a large bowl, add the sugar and lemon zest and set aside.

Place the eggs, lemon curd and sour cream into the bowl of a stand mixer fitted with a whisk attachment (or use a hand-held electric whisk) and whisk, until fully combined. Pour this into the flour mixture and add the melted butter. Mix until smooth and all ingredients are incorporated, then add the poppy seeds and give the batter a final mix.

Using an ice cream scoop, divide the mixture between the muffin cases, filling to almost two-thirds full. Bake in the preheated oven for 20–25 minutes, until well risen and a skewer inserted into the cakes comes out clean. Transfer to a wire rack and, while still warm, prick the cupcakes all over with a cocktail stick/toothpick in readiness for the lemon syrup.

To make the syrup, place the lemon juice and sugar in a small saucepan and warm gently until the sugar has melted. Remove from the heat.

Using a teaspoon, spoon the warm syrup over each cake, until all the syrup has been absorbed into the cakes. Allow the cupcakes to cool completely before icing.

To make the buttercream, place the butter into the bowl of a stand mixer fitted with a paddle attachment (or use a hand-held electric whisk), and beat until soft and fluffy. Sift in half of the icing/confectioners' sugar and slowly mix until incorporated. Add the second half of the sugar, then beat, slowly, until all the sugar has been incorporated. Add the lemon curd, then add the milk, a tablespoon at a time, mixing until light and fluffy at medium speed. If the buttercream is too stiff, add a little more milk.

Spoon the buttercream into the piping/pastry bag, and pipe a swirl onto the top of each cupcake. Alternatively, spread the buttercream onto each cake using a palette knife or metal spatula.

Decorate each cupcake with some freshly grated lemon zest, a drizzle of lemon curd and a sprinkling of poppy seeds.

blueberry cupcake

THIS BLUEBERRY-SPECKLED VANILLA SPONGE IS PERFECTLY COMPLEMENTED BY A
MOREISH BLUEBERRY CREAM CHEESE ICING MADE WITH FRESH BLUEBERRY PURÉE.

200 g self-raising flour/1 1/2
  cups cake flour mixed with
  3 teaspoons baking powder
1 teaspoon baking powder
175 g/1 1/2 sticks butter
250 g/1 1/4 cups caster/
  granulated sugar
1 1/2 teaspoons vanilla bean
  paste
3 eggs
175 ml/2/3 cup sour cream
48 blueberries

CREAM CHEESE ICING
60 g/1/2 cup blueberries
1 teaspoon caster/granulated
  sugar
1 quantity Basic Cream
  Cheese Icing (see page 21)

TO DECORATE
36 fresh blueberries

muffin pan lined with
  12 muffin cases

piping/pastry bag fitted with
  a large star nozzle/tip

MAKES 12

Preheat the oven to 180°C (350°F) Gas 4.

Sift the flour and baking powder into a bowl and set aside.

Place the butter and sugar into the bowl of a stand mixer fitted with a paddle attachment (or use a hand-held electric whisk) and beat the mixture at medium speed for 1–2 minutes, until light and fluffy. Occasionally stop to scrape down the sides of the bowl with a rubber spatula to make sure that all the butter and sugar is incorporated.

Add the vanilla bean paste and mix. Slowly add the eggs, one at a time, mixing at low speed, until incorporated. Add the sifted dry ingredients and mix at low speed until combined. Scrape down the sides of the bowl with a rubber spatula. Once the batter is smooth, add the sour cream and mix until incorporated. Do not over-mix.

Using an ice cream scoop, divide the mixture between the muffin cases, filling to almost two-thirds full. Very gently push four blueberries into the batter of each cake. Bake in the preheated oven for 20–25 minutes, until well risen and a skewer inserted into the cakes comes out clean. Transfer to a wire rack to cool completely.

For the cream cheese icing, simmer the blueberries in a saucepan with the caster/granulated sugar and 1 teaspoon water for 10 minutes, then blend until smooth. Set aside and allow to cool. Prepare the Basic Cream Cheese Icing following the instructions on page 21. Slowly combine the icing with the cooled blueberry purée.

To decorate, spoon the cream cheese icing into the piping/pastry bag, and pipe a swirl onto the top of each cupcake. Alternatively, spread the buttercream onto each cake using a palette knife or metal spatula. Finish each cupcake with 3 blueberries.

sugar-free blueberry cupcake

IF YOU ARE AVOIDING SUGAR, THEN THIS IS THE GUILT-FREE CUPCAKE FOR YOU.
IT HAS ALL THE CHARACTERISTICS OF OUR REGULAR BLUEBERRY CUPCAKE.

200 g self-raising flour/1 ½
    cups cake flour mixed with
    3 teaspoons baking powder
1 teaspoon baking powder
200 g/1 cup xylitol
3 eggs
175 g/1 ½ sticks butter, melted
1 ½ teaspoons vanilla bean
    paste
175 ml/²⁄₃ cup sour cream
36 fresh blueberries

CREAM CHEESE ICING
60 g/½ stick butter
1 teaspoon vanilla bean paste
400 g/14 oz. full-fat cream
    cheese
2 tablespoons agave nectar

TO DECORATE
36 fresh blueberries

muffin pan lined with
    12 muffin cases

piping/pastry bag fitted with
    a large star nozzle/tip

MAKES 12

Preheat the oven to 180°C (350°F) Gas 4.

Sift the flour and baking powder into a large bowl and stir in the xylitol. Set aside.

Place the eggs, melted butter and vanilla bean paste into the bowl of a stand mixer fitted with a paddle attachment (or use a hand-held electric whisk) and beat the mixture at medium speed for 1–2 minutes, until light and fluffy.

Add the dry ingredients and mix at low speed, until combined. Scrape down the sides of the bowl with a rubber spatula. Once the batter is smooth, add the sour cream and mix until incorporated. Do not over-mix.

Using an ice cream scoop, divide the mixture between the muffin cases, filling to almost two-thirds full. Very gently push three blueberries into the batter of each cake. Bake in the preheated oven for 20–25 minutes, until well risen and a skewer inserted into the cakes comes out clean. Transfer to a wire rack to cool completely.

To make the cream cheese icing, place the butter into the bowl of a stand mixer fitted with a paddle attachment (or use a hand-held electric whisk), and beat until smooth and soft. Add the vanilla bean paste and cream cheese, and beat at medium to high speed, until smooth and glossy. Finally, add the agave nectar and slowly mix to combine. Do not over-mix.

To decorate, spoon the icing into the piping/pastry bag, and pipe a swirl onto the top of each cupcake. Alternatively, spread the cream cheese icing onto each cake using a palette knife or metal spatula. Finish each cupcake with 3 blueberries.

Replacing refined sugar with xylitol and agave nectar turns this cupcake into a delicious guilt-free treat.

mango cupcake

MANGO LOVERS WILL ADORE THIS CUPCAKE! IT HAS A VANILLA BASE SPIKED WITH
MANGO AND A MANGO PURÉE CORE, TOPPED OFF WITH COOL CREAM CHEESE ICING.

200 g self-raising flour/
   1½ cups cake flour mixed
   with 3 teaspoons baking
   powder
1 teaspoon baking powder
175 g/1½ sticks butter
250 g/1¼ cups caster/
   granulated sugar
1 teaspoons vanilla bean paste
grated zest from 1 orange
3 eggs
175 g/²/₃ cup sour cream
100 g/²/₃ cup chopped ripe
   fresh mango

MANGO PURÉE CORE
150 g/1 cup chopped ripe
   fresh mango
1 tablespoon freshly squeezed
   orange juice

CREAM CHEESE ICING
70 g/²/₃ stick butter
1 teaspoon vanilla bean paste
180 g/1¼ cups icing/
   confectioners' sugar
400 g/14 oz. full-fat cream
   cheese

Preheat the oven to 180°C (350°F) Gas 4.

Sift the flour and baking powder into a bowl and set aside.

Place the butter and sugar into the bowl of a stand mixer fitted
with a paddle attachment (or use a hand-held electric whisk) and beat
the mixture at medium speed for 1–2 minutes, until light and fluffy.
Occasionally stop to scrape down the sides of the bowl with a rubber
spatula to make sure that all the butter and sugar is incorporated.

Add the vanilla bean paste and orange zest, and mix. Then, on low
speed, add the eggs, one at a time, mixing until the eggs are fully
incorporated. Slowly add the sifted dry ingredients into the egg mixture
on a low speed until combined. Scrape down the sides of the bowl with
a rubber spatula. Once the batter is smooth, add the sour cream and mix
until incorporated. Do not over-mix. Fold the chopped mango through
the batter.

Using an ice cream scoop, divide the mixture between the muffin
cases, filling to almost two-thirds full. Bake in the preheated oven for
20–25 minutes, until well risen and a skewer inserted into the cakes
comes out clean. Transfer to a wire rack to cool completely.

To make the mango purée core, place the mango and orange juice
into a blender or food processor and blend until smooth.

Once the cupcakes are cool, use a sharp knife or apple corer
to remove a small section from the centre of each cupcake. Set aside
1 tablespoon of the mango purée for the buttercream, then, using a
teaspoon (or disposable piping/pastry bag), fill the holes almost to the
top with the remaining purée.

To make the cream cheese icing, place the butter into the bowl of a stand mixer fitted with a paddle attachment (or use a hand-held electric whisk), and beat until smooth and soft. Add the vanilla bean paste and sift in the icing/confectioners' sugar. Add the cream cheese and beat at medium to high speed for 30 seconds, until smooth and glossy. Do not over-mix. Carefully fold through the reserved tablespoon of mango purée; it can look very pretty if you leave this slightly rippled through the icing.

Spoon the cream cheese icing into the piping/pastry bag and pipe a swirl onto each cupcake. Alternatively, spread the icing onto each cupcake using a palette knife or metal spatula. Decorate the cupcakes with the fresh fruit.

passion fruit cupcake

THIS CUPCAKE LOOKS BEAUTIFUL WITH ITS GOLDEN, TANGY PASSION FRUIT ICING AND MOIST VANILLA SPONGE, WHICH HIDES A CUSTARD AND MASCARPONE CORE.

200 g self-raising flour/1 1/2
    cups cake flour mixed with
    3 teaspoons baking powder
1 teaspoon baking powder
175 g/1 1/2 sticks butter
250 g/1 1/4 cups caster/
    granulated sugar
1 1/2 teaspoons vanilla bean
    paste
3 eggs
175 ml/2/3 cup sour cream

CUSTARD CORE
75 g/3 oz. mascarpone cheese
150 ml/1/2 cup store-bought
    vanilla custard
pulp and seeds of 1 passion
    fruit

BUTTERCREAM
150 g/1 1/4 sticks butter
350 g/3 cups icing/
    confectioners' sugar
2 tablespoons sieved/strained
    passion fruit pulp

TO DECORATE
fresh passion fruit pulp

muffin pan lined with
    12 muffin cases

piping/pastry bag fitted with
    a large star nozzle/tip

MAKES 12

Preheat the oven to 180°C (350°F) Gas 4.

Sift the flour and baking powder into a bowl and set aside.

Place the butter and sugar into the bowl of a stand mixer fitted with a paddle attachment (or use a hand-held electric whisk) and beat the mixture at medium speed for 1–2 minutes, until light and fluffy. Occasionally scrape down the sides of the bowl with a rubber spatula to make sure that all the butter and sugar is incorporated.

Add the vanilla bean paste and mix. On low speed, add the eggs, one at a time, until fully incorporated into the mixture. Add the sifted dry ingredients, mixing on low speed until combined. Scrape down the sides of the bowl with a rubber spatula. Once the batter is smooth, add the sour cream and mix until smooth. Do not over-mix.

Using an ice cream scoop, divide the mixture between the muffin cases, filling to almost two-thirds full. Bake in the preheated oven for 20–25 minutes, until well risen and a skewer inserted into the cakes comes out clean. Transfer to a wire rack to cool completely.

For the custard filling, place the mascarpone and custard into the bowl of a stand mixer fitted with a paddle attachment (or use a hand-held electric whisk) and beat the mixture at medium speed for 1 minute, until well blended. Add the passion fruit and mix until smooth.

To make the buttercream, place the butter into the bowl of a stand mixer fitted with a paddle attachment (or use a hand-held electric whisk), and beat until soft and fluffy. Sift in half of the icing/confectioners' sugar and slowly mix until incorporated. Add the second half of the sugar, then beat, slowly, until all the sugar has been incorporated. Slowly add the sieved/strained passion fruit, a tablespoon at a time, mixing at a medium speed, until the buttercream is light and fluffy.

To assemble the cupcakes, use a sharp knife or apple corer to remove a small section from the centre of each cooled cupcake. Using a teaspoon (or disposable piping/pastry bag), fill the holes almost to the top with the custard filling.

Spoon the buttercream into the piping/pastry bag, and pipe a swirl onto the top of each cupcake. Alternatively, spread the buttercream onto each cake using a palette knife or metal spatula. Decorate each cupcake with fresh passion fruit pulp.

lactose-free strawberry cupcake

250 g/1¾ cups plain/
  all-purpose flour
1 teaspoon bicarbonate
  of soda/baking soda
½ teaspoon baking powder
a pinch of salt
150 g/⅔ cup lactose-free
  butter
250 g/1 cup caster/
  granulated sugar
2 teaspoons vanilla bean paste
2 eggs
150 ml/⅔ cup lactose-free
  full-fat/whole milk
125 ml/½ cup lactose-free
  strawberry yogurt

BUTTERCREAM
175 g/¾ cup lactose-free
  butter
1 teaspoon vanilla bean paste
400 g/3½ cups icing/
  confectioners' sugar
60 g/¼ cup fresh strawberries,
  mashed

TO DECORATE
sliced fresh strawberries

*muffin pan lined with
  12 muffin cases*

*piping/pastry bag fitted with
  a large star nozzle/tip*

MAKES 12

Preheat the oven to 180°C (350°F) Gas 4.

Sift the flour, bicarbonate of soda/baking soda, baking powder and salt into a large bowl. Set aside.

Place the butter, sugar and vanilla bean paste into the bowl of a stand mixer fitted with a paddle attachment (or use a hand-held electric whisk) and beat at medium speed for 1–2 minutes, until light and fluffy. Occasionally stop to scrape down the sides of the bowl with a rubber spatula to make sure that all the butter and sugar are incorporated.

With the mixer on low speed, add the eggs, one at a time, mixing until fully incorporated.

Slowly add the dry ingredients, mixing at low speed, until combined. Scrape down the sides of the bowl, and briefly beat at high speed until the mixture is smooth. Add the milk and yogurt, and mix until incorporated. Do not over-mix.

Using an ice cream scoop, divide the mixture between the muffin cases, filling to almost two-thirds full. Bake in the preheated oven for 20–25 minutes, until well risen and a skewer inserted into the cakes comes out clean. Transfer to a wire rack to cool completely.

To make the buttercream, place the butter and vanilla bean paste into the bowl of a stand mixer fitted with a paddle attachment (or use a hand-held electric whisk) and beat until soft and smooth. Sift in half of the icing/confectioners' sugar and, with the mixer on low speed, mix until incorporated. Add the second half of the sugar and beat, still on low speed, until incorporated. Add the mashed strawberries, then briefly mix at medium speed, until the buttercream is light and fluffy.

Spread the buttercream onto each cake using a palette knife or metal spatula. Alternatively, spoon the buttercream into the piping/pastry bag and pipe a swirl of buttercream onto the top of each cupcake. Decorate with slices of fresh strawberry.

THIS MOIST, FRUITY AND VERY
ADDICTIVE RECIPE IS FOR ANYONE
WHO IS LACTOSE-INTOLERANT.

rose and pistachio cupcake

A BEAUTIFULLY FRAGRANT CUPCAKE STUDDED WITH PISTACHIO NUTS AND TOPPED WITH A HEADY ROSE BUTTERCREAM. A LADYLIKE TREAT AND A TASTE OF THE EXOTIC.

175 g self-raising flour/1 1/3
cups cake flour mixed with
2 teaspoons baking powder
1 teaspoon baking powder
125 g/1 1/8 sticks butter
200 g/1 cup caster/
granulated sugar
1 teaspoon vanilla bean paste
3 eggs
1 teaspoon rose water
125 ml/1/2 cup sour cream
50 g/1/4 cup chopped unsalted
pistachio nuts

BUTTERCREAM
150 g/1 1/4 sticks butter
1 teaspoon vanilla bean paste
pink food colouring paste
350 g/3 cups icing/
confectioners' sugar
1 tablespoon rose water
2–3 tablespoons full-fat/
whole milk

TO DECORATE
chopped pistachio nuts and
edible rose petals

muffin pan lined with
12 muffin cases

piping/pastry bag fitted with
a large star nozzle/tip

MAKES 12

Preheat the oven to 180°C (350°F) Gas 4.

Sift the flour and baking powder into a bowl and set aside.

Place the butter, sugar and vanilla bean paste into the bowl of a stand mixer fitted with a paddle attachment (or use a hand-held electric whisk) and beat the mixture at medium speed for 1–2 minutes, until light and fluffy. Occasionally scrape down the sides of the bowl with a rubber spatula to make sure that all the butter and sugar is incorporated.

On low speed, add the eggs, one at a time, until fully incorporated into the mixture. Add the sifted dry ingredients, mixing on low speed, until combined. Scrape down the sides of the bowl with a rubber spatula. Once the batter is smooth, add the rose water, sour cream and pistachios, and mix. Do not over-mix.

Using an ice cream scoop, divide the mixture between the muffin cases, filling to almost two-thirds full. Bake in the preheated oven for 20–25 minutes, until well risen and a skewer inserted into the cakes comes out clean. Transfer the cupcakes to a wire rack to cool completely.

To make the buttercream, place the butter into the bowl of a stand mixer fitted with a paddle attachment (or use a hand-held electric whisk), and beat until soft and fluffy. Add the vanilla bean paste and a small amount of pink food colouring and mix. Sift in half of the icing/confectioners' sugar and slowly mix until incorporated. Add the second half of the sugar, then beat slowly, until all the sugar has been incorporated. Add the rose water, then slowly add the milk, a tablespoonful at a time, mixing at medium speed until the buttercream is light and fluffy. If it is too stiff, add a little more milk.

Spoon the buttercream into the piping/pastry bag, and pipe a swirl onto the top of each cupcake. Alternatively, spread the buttercream onto each cake using a palette knife or metal spatula. Decorate with chopped pistachios and edible rose petals.

elderflower cupcake

A TASTE OF SUMMER! DELICATE ELDERFLOWER SPONGE ENCASES A GOOSEBERRY
AND ELDERFLOWER CENTRE, COMPLETED WITH AN ELDERFLOWER BUTTERCREAM.

200 g self-raising flour/
1½ cups cake flour mixed
with 3 teaspoons baking
powder
1 teaspoon baking powder
175 g/1½ sticks butter
250 g/1¼ cups caster/
granulated sugar
1½ teaspoons vanilla bean
paste
3 eggs
175 ml/⅔ cup sour cream
3½ tablespoons elderflower
cordial

FILLING
150 g/½ cup gooseberry
jam/jelly
2 tablespoons elderflower
cordial

BUTTERCREAM
150 g/1¼ sticks butter
½ teaspoon vanilla bean paste
350 g/3 cups icing/
confectioners' sugar
3 tablespoons elderflower
cordial

Preheat the oven to 180°C (350°F) Gas 4.

Sift the flour and baking powder into a bowl and set aside.

Place the butter and sugar into the bowl of a stand mixer fitted with
a paddle attachment (or use a hand-held electric whisk) and beat the
mixture at medium speed for 1–2 minutes, until light and fluffy.
Occasionally scrape down the sides of the bowl with a rubber spatula
to make sure that all the butter and sugar is incorporated.

Add the vanilla bean paste and mix. On low speed, add the eggs,
one at a time, until fully incorporated. Add the sifted dry ingredients,
mixing on low speed until combined. Scrape down the sides of the bowl
with a rubber spatula. Once the batter is smooth, add the sour cream
and elderflower cordial, and mix until smooth. Do not over-mix.

Using an ice cream scoop, divide the mixture between the muffin
cases, filling to almost two-thirds full. Bake in the preheated oven for
20–25 minutes, until well risen and a skewer inserted into the cakes
comes out clean. Transfer to a wire rack to cool completely.

To make the filling, combine the gooseberry jam/jelly and elderflower
cordial in a small bowl and set aside.

To make the buttercream, put the butter and vanilla bean paste
into the bowl of a stand mixer fitted with a paddle attachment (or use
a hand-held electric whisk), and beat until soft and fluffy. Sift in half of the
icing/confectioners' sugar and slowly mix until incorporated. Add the
second half of the sugar, then beat, slowly, until all the sugar has been
incorporated. Add the cordial, a tablespoon at a time, mixing at
medium speed, until the icing is light and fluffy. If the icing is too stiff,
add a little milk.

To assemble the cupcakes, use a sharp knife or apple corer to remove a small section from the centre of each cooled cupcake. Using a teaspoon (or disposable piping/pastry bag), fill the holes almost to the top with the filling.

Spoon the buttercream into the piping/pastry bag, and pipe a swirl onto the top of each cupcake. Alternatively, spread the buttercream onto each cake using a palette knife or metal spatula. Decorate with gooseberry jam/jelly or leftover filling.

SUGAR AND SPICE

GINGER CUPCAKE

MAPLE SYRUP CUPCAKE

PECAN PIE CUPCAKE

MINCE PIE CUPCAKE

ginger cupcake

LOOKING FOR SOMETHING A LITTLE BIT SPICY TO CHEER UP A GREY WINTER'S DAY? THIS CUPCAKE USES A COMBINATION OF DRIED AND STEM GINGER TO GIVE A GLORIOUS BACKGROUND WARMTH, AND IS FINISHED WITH A CINNAMON CREAM CHEESE ICING. WHO SAID THAT THERE ISN'T A CUPCAKE FOR EVERY SEASON!

175 g self-raising flour/1 1/3 cups cake flour mixed with 3 teaspoons baking powder
3/4 teaspoon baking powder
1 1/2 teaspoons ground ginger
125 g/1 1/8 sticks butter
100 g/1/2 cup caster/granulated sugar
100 g/1/2 cup soft light brown sugar
1 teaspoon vanilla bean paste
3 eggs
50 g/1/4 cup chopped preserved stem ginger
125 ml/1/2 cup sour cream

GANACHE CORE
120 ml/1/2 cup double/heavy cream
80 g/1/2 cup chopped dark/bittersweet chocolate (up to 60% cocoa solids)

Preheat the oven to 180°C (350°F) Gas 4.

Sift the flour, baking powder and ground ginger into a bowl. Set aside.

Place the butter, sugars and vanilla bean paste into the bowl of a stand mixer fitted with a paddle attachment (or use a hand-held electric whisk), and beat the mixture at medium to high speed for 1–2 minutes, until light and fluffy. Occasionally stop to scrape down the sides of the bowl with a rubber spatula to make sure that all the butter and sugar is incorporated.

Mixing at low speed, add the eggs, one at a time, beating until incorporated. Scrape down the sides of the bowl with a rubber spatula, and mix again.

With the speed set to low, slowly add the sifted dry ingredients. Scrape down the sides of the bowl with a rubber spatula, and briefly beat at high speed until the mixture is smooth. Fold in the preserved stem ginger and the sour cream. Do not over-mix.

Using an ice cream scoop, divide the mixture between the muffin cases, filling to almost two-thirds full. Bake in the preheated oven for 20–23 minutes, until well risen and a skewer inserted into the cakes comes out clean. Transfer to a wire rack to cool completely.

To make the ganache core, place the double/heavy cream in a small saucepan and heat until almost at boiling point. Place the chopped

CREAM CHEESE ICING

60 g/½ stick butter
1 teaspoon vanilla bean paste
¼ teaspoon ground cinnamon
½ teaspoon ground ginger
175 g/1½ cups icing/
  confectioners' sugar
400 g/14 oz. full-fat cream
  cheese
½ tablespoon syrup from the
  preserved stem ginger jar

TO DECORATE

dark/bittersweet chocolate
  curls

*muffin pan lined with
  12 muffin cases*

MAKES 12

chocolate in a heatproof bowl. Pour the hot cream over the chopped chocolate and stir to combine. The mixture will be smooth and glossy. Allow to cool before placing in the refrigerator to set.

To make the cream cheese icing, place the butter into the bowl of a stand mixer fitted with a paddle attachment (or use a hand-held electric whisk), and beat until smooth and soft. Add the vanilla bean paste, cinnamon and ginger, and sift in the icing/confectioners' sugar. Add the cream cheese and beat at medium to high speed for about 30 seconds, until smooth and glossy. Do not over-mix.

To assemble the cupcakes, use a sharp knife or apple corer to remove a small section from the centre of each cupcake. Using a teaspoon (or disposable piping/pastry bag), fill the holes almost to the top with ganache.

Spread the icing onto the cupcakes using a palette knife or metal spatula, and decorate with dark/bittersweet chocolate curls.

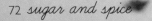

maple syrup cupcake

THIS CUPCAKE HAS BECOME A FIRM FAVOURITE WITH THE LOLA'S TEAM. A MOIST, MAPLE-SCENTED SPONGE IS TOPPED OFF WITH AN ALMOST TOFFEE-LIKE MAPLE BUTTERCREAM. THIS IS THE KIND OF CUPCAKE THAT IS PERFECT TO EAT BY THE FIRE ON A CRISP AUTUMNAL DAY. BE SURE TO USE A GOOD-QUALITY PURE MAPLE SYRUP.

300 g/2¼ cups plain/ all-purpose flour
1¼ teaspoons baking powder
¾ teaspoon bicarbonate soda/baking soda
½ teaspoon ground ginger
75 g/¾ stick butter
60 g/⅓ cup soft light brown sugar
1 teaspoon vanilla bean paste
1 egg
200 ml/1 cup good-quality pure maple syrup (do not use maple-flavoured syrup)
80 ml/⅓ cup sour cream

Preheat the oven to 180°C (350°F) Gas 4.

Sift the flour, baking powder, bicarbonate of soda/baking soda and ground ginger into a bowl and set aside.

Place the butter and sugar into the bowl of a stand mixer fitted with a paddle attachment (or use a hand-held electric whisk), and beat the mixture at medium to high speed for 1–2 minutes, until light and fluffy. Occasionally stop to scrape down the sides of the bowl with a rubber spatula to make sure that all the butter and sugar is incorporated.

Mixing at low speed, add the egg and maple syrup, beating slowly until fully incorporated. Scrape down the sides of the bowl with a rubber spatula, and mix again.

With the speed set to low, slowly add the sifted dry ingredients and the sour cream. Beat until all the ingredients have been combined and the batter is smooth. Scrape down the sides of the bowl with a rubber spatula, and mix again.

Using an ice cream scoop, divide the mixture between the muffin cases, filling to almost two-thirds full. Bake in the preheated oven for 20–25 minutes, until well risen and a skewer inserted into the cakes comes out clean. Transfer to a wire rack to cool completely.

BUTTERCREAM
150 g/1¼ sticks butter
60 g/2¼ oz. full-fat cream
  cheese
80 g/½ cup soft dark brown
  sugar
1 teaspoon vanilla bean paste
120 ml/½ cup good-quality
  pure maple syrup
160 g/1⅓ cups icing/
  confectioners' sugar

TO DECORATE
12 pecan halves
pure maple syrup, to drizzle

*muffin pan lined with
  12 muffin cases*

*piping/pastry bag fitted with
  a large star nozzle/tip*

MAKES 12

To make the buttercream, place the butter, cream cheese and soft dark brown sugar into the bowl of a stand mixer fitted with a paddle attachment (or use a hand-held electric whisk), and beat until soft and fluffy. Add the vanilla bean paste and maple syrup and mix again, until combined. Sift in half of the icing/confectioners' sugar and, with the mixer on a low speed, mix until incorporated. Add the second half of the sugar, then beat slowly, until all the sugar has been incorporated and the buttercream is light and fluffy. Cover with clingfilm/plastic wrap and place in the refrigerator for at least 1 hour.

Spoon the buttercream into the piping/pastry bag and pipe a swirl onto each cupcake. Alternatively, spread the buttercream onto each cupcake using a palette knife or metal spatula. Decorate each cake with a pecan half and a drizzle of maple syrup.

pecan pie cupcake

THE CLASSIC PECAN PIE HAS BEEN TRANSFORMED INTO A SUMPTUOUS SPICED SPONGE. TOPPED WITH A CREAM CHEESE ICING AND SHARDS OF THE MOST MOREISH PECAN BRITTLE – WE URGE YOU TO TRY THIS STICKY TREAT! STORE ANY LEFTOVER PECAN BRITTLE AWAY FROM MOISTURE IN AN AIR-TIGHT CONTAINER TO KEEP IT CRUNCHY.

200 g self-raising flour/1 1/2 cups cake flour mixed with 3 teaspoons baking powder
1 teaspoon baking powder
a pinch of ground cloves
a pinch of ground cinnamon
125 g/1 1/8 sticks butter
100 g/1/2 cup caster/granulated sugar
100 g/1/2 cup soft dark brown sugar
1 teaspoon vanilla bean paste
2 eggs
60 g/1/2 cup chopped pecan nuts
75 ml/1/3 cup sour cream

Preheat the oven to 180°C (350°F) Gas 4.

Sift the flour, baking powder and ground cloves and ground cinnamon into a mixing bowl, and set aside.

Place the butter, sugars and vanilla bean paste into the bowl of a stand mixer fitted with a paddle attachment (or use a hand-held electric whisk), and beat the mixture at medium to high speed for 1–2 minutes, until light and fluffy. Occasionally stop to scrape down the sides of the bowl with a rubber spatula to make sure that all the butter and sugar is incorporated.

Mixing at low speed, add the eggs, one at a time, beating until incorporated. Scrape down the sides of the bowl with a rubber spatula, and mix again.

With the speed set to low, slowly add the sifted dry ingredients. Scrape down the side of the bowl with a rubber spatula, and briefly beat at high speed until the mixture is smooth. Fold in the chopped pecan nuts and the sour cream. Do not over-mix.

Using an ice cream scoop, divide the mixture between the muffin cases, filling to almost two-thirds full. Bake in the preheated oven for 20–25 minutes, until well risen and a skewer inserted into the cakes comes out clean. Transfer to a wire rack to cool completely.

To make the pecan praline, place the sugar into a heavy-bottomed

PECAN PRALINE
100 g/½ cup caster/
   granulated sugar
60 g/½ cup pecan halves

CREAM CHEESE ICING
1 quantity Basic Cream
   Cheese Icing (see page 21)

muffin pan lined with
   12 muffin cases

baking sheet lined with baking
   parchment

piping/pastry bag fitted with
   a large star nozzle/tip

MAKES 12

saucepan and heat gently over medium heat until the sugar starts
to melt around the edges and turn an amber colour. Do not stir.

Carefully, as the sugar will be very hot, swirl the pan around
to encourage all the sugar to melt and caramelize. Gently bubble the
caramel until the liquid is an even golden brown colour, then remove
from the heat and add the pecans. Swirl the mixture to coat the nuts
in the caramel and then pour onto the lined baking sheet in a thin layer.
Leave to cool and set.

Prepare the Basic Cream Cheese Icing following the instructions on
page 21.

Spoon the cream cheese icing into the piping/pastry bag and pipe a
swirl onto each cupcake. Alternatively, spread the icing onto each cupcake
using a palette knife or metal spatula. To decorate the cupcakes, cut the
pecan brittle into small shards using a sharp knife, then arrange a few
pieces on top of each cupcake.

*The trick with this decoration is not to
worry about being overly neat, placing the
brittle haphazardly into the icing makes for
a dramatic effect.*

min

AT LOI
FES

e pie cupcake

S WE LOVE A GOOD MINCE PIE, SO WE RECREATED THE FLAVOURS IN THIS
VE CUPCAKE. YOU CAN CHOOSE TO ADD THE OPTIONAL DRIED FRUIT TO YOUR
MIXTURE AND THIS WILL GIVE A RICHER 'FRUITCAKE' STYLE CUPCAKE.

140 g self-raising flour/
   1 cup cake flour mixed with
   2 teaspoons baking powder
³/₄ teaspoon baking powder
¹/₂ teaspoon ground ginger
¹/₂ teaspoon ground cinnamon
¹/₄ teaspoon ground nutmeg
a pinch of ground cloves
150 g/1 ¹/₄ sticks butter
75 g/¹/₃ cup soft light brown
   sugar
75 g/¹/₃ cup soft dark brown
   sugar
1 tablespoon grated orange
   zest
3 eggs
175 g/¹/₂ cup good-quality
   traditional mincemeat
150 g/1 cup mixed dried fruit
   (optional)

Start by making the shortbread decorations. Put the sugar and flour
into a bowl and rub in the butter with your fingertips, until the mixture
is a sandy consistency. When you can feel the crumbs sticking together,
gently squeeze the mixture into a ball, wrap it in clingfilm/plastic wrap
and place in the refrigerator for at least 30 minutes.

Preheat the oven to 190°C (375°F) Gas 5.

Once it has rested, roll out the dough on a flour-dusted surface, and
use the mini cookie cutter to cut shapes out of the dough. Place on the
lined baking sheet and bake in the preheated oven for 10–15 minutes
or until a light golden colour. Allow to cool, then dust each piece
of shortbread with edible glitter.

Reduce the oven temperature to 180°C (350°F) Gas 4.

To make the cupcakes, sift the flour, baking powder and spices into
a bowl, and set aside.

Place the butter, sugars and orange zest into the bowl of a stand
mixer fitted with a paddle attachment (or use a hand-held electric whisk),
and beat the mixture at medium to high speed for 1–2 minutes, until light
and fluffy.

Mixing on low speed, add the eggs, one at a time, making sure you
stop to scrape down the sides of the bowl with a rubber spatula. Add
the mincemeat and mix until fully combined. With the speed set to low,
slowly add the sifted dry ingredients, and mix until fully combined. If
you are including the dried fruit, add it at this stage and give the batter
a thorough mix.

SHORTBREAD
40 g/3 $\frac{1}{4}$ tablespoons
   caster/granulated sugar
140 g/1 cup plain/
   all-purpose flour
110 g/1 stick butter
edible gold glitter

CREAM CHEESE ICING
60 g/$\frac{1}{2}$ stick butter
1 teaspoon vanilla bean paste
$\frac{1}{2}$ teaspoon ground cinnamon
175 g/1 $\frac{1}{2}$ cups icing/
   confectioners' sugar
400 g/14 oz. full-fat cream
   cheese

Using an ice cream scoop, divide the mixture between the muffin cases, filling to almost two-thirds full. Bake in the preheated oven for 20–25 minutes, until well risen and a skewer inserted into the cakes comes out clean. Transfer to a wire rack to cool completely.

To make the cream cheese icing, place the butter into the bowl of a stand mixer fitted with a paddle attachment (or use a hand-held electric whisk), and beat until smooth. Add the vanilla bean paste and ground cinnamon, and sift in the icing/confectioners' sugar. Add the cream cheese

mini cookie cutters in
 the shapes of your choice

baking sheet lined with baking
 parchment

muffin pan lined with
 12 muffin cases

piping/pastry bag fitted with
 a large star nozzle/tip

MAKES 12

and beat at medium to high speed for about 30 seconds, until smooth and glossy. Do not over-mix.

Spoon the cream cheese icing into the piping/pastry bag and pipe swirls of icing onto the top of each cupcake. Alternatively, spread the icing onto the top of each cupcake using a palette knife or metal spatula. Decorate each cupcake with the shortbread shapes.

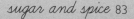

COOKIES AND CANDIES

COOKIES AND CREAM CUPCAKE

CUSTARD CREAM CUPCAKE

CHOCOLATE HAZELNUT CUPCAKE

PEANUT BUTTER CUPCAKE

BLUE MONSTER CUPCAKE

RAINBOW SWIRL CUPCAKE

RHUBARB AND CUSTARD CUPCAKE

JAMMY DODGER CUPCAKE

SNOWMAN CUPCAKE

HIGH HAT MARSHMALLOW CUPCAKE

cookies and cream cupcake

AT LOLA'S WE WONDERED IF WE COULD TURN THE ICONIC CHOCOLATE SANDWICH COOKIE INTO A DELICIOUS CUPCAKE. WE THINK WE HAVE SUCCEEDED! WE ADD OREO CRUMBS TO THE CAKE BATTER AND BUTTERCREAM TO GIVE THAT CLASSIC FLAVOUR, BUT IN CUPCAKE FORM. WE TOP THE CUPCAKES OFF WITH CUTE MINI SANDWICH COOKIES.

175 g self-raising flour/1 1/3 cups cake flour mixed with 3 teaspoons baking powder
3/4 teaspoon baking powder
125 g/1 1/8 sticks butter
200 g/1 cup caster/granulated sugar
1 teaspoon vanilla bean paste
3 eggs
150 ml/3/4 cup sour cream
60 g/2 oz. chocolate sandwich biscuits/cookies (such as Oreos), blitzed to crumbs in a food processor

BUTTERCREAM
150 g/1 1/4 sticks butter
1 teaspoon vanilla bean paste
300 g/2 1/2 cups icing/confectioners' sugar
60 ml/1/4 cup full-fat/whole milk

Preheat the oven to 180°C (350°F) Gas 4.

Sift the flour and baking powder into a bowl and set aside.

Place the butter and sugar into the bowl of a stand mixer fitted with a paddle attachment (or use a hand-held electric whisk), and beat the mixture at medium to high speed for 1–2 minutes, until light and fluffy.

Add the vanilla bean paste and mix. Mixing on low speed, add the eggs, one at a time, beating until incorporated.

Slowly add the sifted dry ingredients, and mix on low speed until combined. Scrape down the sides of the bowl with a rubber spatula, and briefly beat at high speed until the mixture is smooth. Add the sour cream and mix until incorporated. Do not over-mix. Stir in the Oreo cookie crumbs.

Using an ice cream scoop, divide the mixture between the muffin cases, filling to almost two-thirds full. Bake in the preheated oven for 18–22 minutes, until well risen and a skewer inserted into the cakes comes out clean. Transfer to a wire rack to cool completely.

To make the buttercream, place the butter into the bowl of a stand mixer fitted with a paddle attachment (or use a hand-held electric whisk), and beat until soft and fluffy. Add the vanilla bean paste and mix again, until combined. Sift in half of the icing/confectioners' sugar and mix on low speed until incorporated. Add the second half of the sugar, then beat

30 g/1 oz. chocolate sandwich
    biscuits/cookies (such as
    Oreos), blitzed to crumbs
    in a food processor

TO DECORATE
12 mini chocolate sandwich
    biscuits/cookies (such as
    Oreos)

*muffin pan lined with
    12 muffin cases*

*piping/pastry bag fitted with
    a large star nozzle/tip*

MAKES 12

slowly until all the sugar is incorporated. Add the milk and Oreo
crumbs, a little at a time, mixing at medium speed, until light and fluffy.
Give it a final fast beat. If the icing is stiff, add a little more milk.

Spoon the buttercream into the piping/pastry bag, and pipe a swirl
of buttercream onto each cake. Alternatively, spread the buttercream
onto each cake using a palette knife or metal spatula. Decorate each
cupcake with a mini chocolate sandwich/biscuit.

custard cream cupcake

USING OUR CLASSIC VANILLA CUPCAKE BASE WE HAVE CREATED THIS DELICIOUS CUSTARD CREAM CAKE. IT HAS A SMOOTH CUSTARD CORE AND A CUSTARD CREAM CRUMB BUTTERCREAM (TRY SAYING THAT WITH YOUR MOUTH FULL!). THE WHOLE THING IS FINISHED WITH AN ICONIC BISCUIT/COOKIE NESTLED IN THE BUTTERCREAM.

200 g self-raising flour/1 1/2 cups cake flour mixed with 3 teaspoons baking powder
1 teaspoon baking powder
175 g/1 1/2 sticks butter
250 g/1 1/4 cup caster/ granulated sugar
1 1/2 teaspoons vanilla bean paste
3 eggs
175 ml/3/4 cup sour cream

CUSTARD CORE
250 ml/1 cup full-fat/ whole milk
3 tablespoons double/heavy cream
1 teaspoon vanilla bean paste
2 egg yolks
1 tablespoon caster/ granulated sugar
2 teaspoons cornflour/ cornstarch

Preheat the oven to 180°C (350°F) Gas 4.

Sift the flour and baking powder into a mixing bowl, and set aside.

Place the butter, sugar and vanilla bean paste into the bowl of a stand mixer fitted with a paddle attachment (or use a hand-held electric whisk), and beat the mixture at medium to high speed for about 2 minutes, until light and fluffy. Scrape down the sides of the bowl with a rubber spatula.

Mixing at low speed, add the eggs, one at a time, beating until incorporated.

Slowly add the sifted dry ingredients, and mix on low speed until combined. Scrape down the side of the bowl with a rubber spatula, and briefly beat at high speed until the mixture is smooth. Add the sour cream and mix until incorporated. Do not over-mix.

Using an ice cream scoop, divide the mixture between the muffin cases, filling to almost two-thirds full. Bake in the preheated oven for 20–25 minutes, until well risen and a skewer inserted into the cakes comes out clean. Transfer to a wire rack to cool completely.

To make the custard core, place the milk, cream and vanilla bean paste in a saucepan, and bring to simmering point slowly over low heat. In a separate bowl, blend the egg yolks, sugar and cornflour/cornstarch until combined. Slowly pour the hot milk over the egg yolk mixture and whisk constantly. Pour the mixture back into the saucepan and heat gently, stirring constantly, until the custard has thickened. Pour the custard into a bowl, cover the surface with clingfilm/plastic wrap, and allow to cool.

BUTTERCREAM

150 g/1 1/4 sticks butter

1 teaspoon vanilla bean paste

300 g/2 1/2 cups icing/
confectioners' sugar

75 ml/1/3 cup full-fat/whole
milk

60 g/2 oz. custard cream
biscuits/sandwich cookies
with vanilla cream filling,
crumbled (about 5 biscuits)

TO DECORATE

6 custard cream
biscuits/sandwich cookies,
with vanilla cream filling,
cut in half

muffin pan lined with
12 muffin cases

piping/pastry bag fitted with
a large star nozzle/tip

MAKES 12

To assemble the cupcakes, use a sharp knife or apple corer to remove a small section from the centre of each cupcake. Using a teaspoon (or disposable piping/pastry bag), fill the holes almost to the top with the cooled custard filling.

To make the buttercream, place the butter into the bowl of a stand mixer fitted with a paddle attachment (or use a hand-held electric whisk), and beat until soft and fluffy. Add the vanilla bean paste and mix again, until combined. Sift in half of the icing/confectioners' sugar and, mixing at low speed, mix until incorporated. Add the second half of the sugar, then beat slowly until all the sugar is incorporated. Add the milk and biscuit/cookie crumbs, a little at a time, mixing at medium speed, until the buttercream is light and fluffy. If the buttercream is too stiff, add a little more milk.

Spoon the buttercream into the piping/pastry bag, and pipe a swirl of buttercream onto each cupcake. Alternatively, spread the buttercream onto each cake using a palette knife or metal spatula.

Decorate each cupcake with a biscuit/sandwich cookie half.

chocolate hazelnut cupcake

A GREAT WAY TO GET YOUR CHOCOLATE HAZELNUT FIX! OUR CLASSIC CHOCOLATE BASE
ENROBES A RICH HAZELNUT CREAM, AND IS FINISHED WITH A MARBLED ICING.

3 eggs
220 g/1 cup plus 2
   tablespoons caster/
   granulated sugar
150 ml/²/₃ cup sunflower oil
80 ml/¹/₃ cup full-fat/whole
   milk
150 g self-raising flour/
   1 cup cake flour mixed with
   2 teaspoons baking powder
45 g/¹/₃ cup unsweetened
   cocoa powder

GANACHE
140 ml/³/₄ cup double/heavy
   cream
75 g/3 oz. plain/semisweet
   chocolate (up to 40% cocoa
   solids)

HAZELNUT CREAM CORE
125 g/¹/₂ cup chocolate
   hazelnut spread
   (such as Nutella)
80 ml/¹/₃ cup double/heavy
   cream

Preheat the oven to 180°C (350°F) Gas 4.

Place the eggs and sugar into the bowl of a stand mixer fitted with
a whisk attachment (or use a hand-held electric whisk), and beat the
mixture at medium to high speed for about 2 minutes, until light and fluffy.
If using a stand mixer, switch to the paddle attachment. Combine the oil
and milk, then slowly add to the egg mixture, and mix just until combined.

Sift the cocoa powder and flour together into a separate bowl, and
add to the batter, a little at a time, beating until incorporated. Scrape
down the sides of the bowl with a rubber spatula, and briefly beat at high
speed until the mixture is smooth. Do not over-mix.

Using an ice cream scoop, divide the mixture between the muffin
cases, filling to almost two-thirds full. Bake in the preheated oven for
20–25 minutes, until well risen and a skewer inserted into the cakes
comes out clean. Transfer to a wire rack to cool completely.

To make the ganache, place the double/heavy cream in a small
saucepan and heat until almost at boiling point. Place the chopped
chocolate in a heatproof bowl. Pour the hot cream over the chocolate
and stir to combine, until smooth and glossy. Allow to cool before placing
in the refrigerator to set.

To make the hazelnut cream core, place the chocolate hazelnut
spread in a small saucepan and warm slightly so that it softens. Remove
from the heat and transfer to a bowl. Add the cream, and stir until
smooth. Set aside to cool.

Topped with a marbled swirl of hazelnut buttercream and dark chocolate ganache, these cupcakes are not for the faint-hearted!

BUTTERCREAM
125 g/1 1/8 sticks butter
180 g/2/3 cup chocolate
  hazelnut spread
  (such as Nutella)
90 g/2/3 cup icing/
  confectioners' sugar

TO DECORATE
30 g/1/4 cup chopped
  hazelnuts

*muffin pan lined with
  12 muffin cases*

*piping/pastry bag fitted with
  a large star nozzle/tip*

MAKES 12

To make the buttercream, place the butter into the bowl of a stand mixer fitted with a paddle attachment (or use a hand-held electric whisk), and beat until soft and fluffy. Place the chocolate hazelnut spread into a small saucepan and gently warm until it has softened, then set aside to cool slightly. Sift in half of the icing/confectioners' sugar and, mixing at low speed, mix until incorporated. Add the second half of the sugar, then beat, slowly, until incorporated. Add the warmed Nutella and mix at medium speed, until combined.

To assemble the cupcakes, use a sharp knife or apple corer to remove a small section from the centre of each cooled cupcake. Using a teaspoon (or disposable piping/pastry bag), fill the holes almost to the top with the hazelnut cream.

Spoon the ganache down one side of the piping/pastry bag and spoon the buttercream down the other side. This will create a marbled effect when piped. Pipe the buttercream and ganache onto each cake in a swirl. Decorate each cupcake with chopped hazelnuts.

peanut butter cupcake

LOLA'S LOVES PEANUT BUTTER, AND HERE WE USE BOTH CRUNCHY AND SMOOTH PEANUT BUTTER TO CREATE A MOIST, NUTTY TREAT. WE HAVE INCLUDED AN OPTIONAL JAM/JELLY CORE TO GET THE CLASSIC AMERICAN 'PEANUT BUTTER AND JELLY' FEEL.

150 g/1¼ sticks butter
175 g/¾ cup soft dark brown sugar
1 teaspoon vanilla bean paste
100 g/½ cup smooth peanut butter
75 g/¼ cup crunchy peanut butter
1 egg
1½ teaspoons baking powder
175 g/1⅓ cups plain/all-purpose flour
150 ml/⅔ cup full-fat/whole milk

Preheat the oven to 180°C (350°F) Gas 4.

Place the butter, sugar and vanilla bean paste into the bowl of a stand mixer fitted with a paddle attachment (or use a hand-held electric whisk), and beat the mixture at medium to high speed for about 2 minutes, until light and fluffy.

Add both the peanut butters to the bowl and mix until incorporated. Add the egg, and beat until combined.

In another bowl, sift together the baking powder and flour. With the mixer on low speed, add half the sifted dry ingredients and half the milk. Repeat with the remaining flour and milk, mixing until the batter is smooth. Do not over-mix.

Using an ice cream scoop, divide the mixture between the muffin cases, filling to almost two-thirds full. Bake in the preheated oven for 25–28 minutes, or until risen and a skewer inserted into the middle comes out clean. Transfer the cupcakes to a wire rack to cool completely.

For the buttercream, place the butter and vanilla bean paste into the bowl of a stand mixer fitted with a paddle attachment (or use a hand-held electric whisk), and beat until smooth and soft. Into another bowl, sift the cocoa powder and icing/confectioners' sugar. Add the sifted cocoa powder and sugar to the butter, a little at a time, mixing slowly,

BUTTERCREAM

110 g/1 stick butter

1 teaspoon vanilla bean
   paste

400 g/scant 3 1/2 cups
   icing/confectioners' sugar,
   sifted

75 g/1/3 cup unsweetened
   cocoa powder

60 ml/1/4 cup full-fat/whole
   milk

100 g/1/3 cup smooth
   peanut butter

JAM/JELLY CORE
(OPTIONAL)

75 g/1/4 cup raspberry
   or strawberry jam/jelly

TO DECORATE
chopped unsalted peanuts

*muffin pan lined with
   12 muffin cases*

*piping/pastry bag fitted with
   a large star nozzle/tip*

MAKES 12

until incorporated. Add the milk, a tablespoonful at a time, mixing at medium speed, until the buttercream is smooth. Beat at high speed, until light and fluffy. If the buttercream is too stiff, add a little more milk to soften. Gently fold in the peanut butter, leaving it slightly rippled.

If you want to add the jam/jelly core, use a sharp knife or apple corer to remove a small section from the centre of each cooled cupcake. Using a teaspoon (or disposable piping/pastry bag), fill the holes almost to the top with raspberry or strawberry jam/jelly.

To decorate, spoon the buttercream into the piping/pastry bag, and pipe a swirl onto the top of each cupcake. Alternatively, spread the buttercream onto each cake using a palette knife or metal spatula. Decorate with chopped peanuts.

This rich cupcake is absolute heaven for peanut butter fans. The chocolate buttercream is rippled through with smooth peanut butter, and the whole thing is sprinkled with extra unsalted peanuts to finish.

blue monster cupcake

NOW FOR SOMETHING FUN! FOR THIS HALLOWEEN CUPCAKE, A SPECIAL NOZZLE/
TIP MAKES SPAGHETTI-LIKE STRANDS OF BUTTERCREAM TO CREATE A MONSTER FACE.

200 g self-raising flour/1¹/₂
   cups cake flour mixed with
   3 teaspoons baking powder
1 teaspoon baking powder
175 g/1¹/₂ sticks butter
250 g/1¹/₄ cups caster/
   granulated sugar
1¹/₂ teaspoons vanilla bean
   paste
3 eggs
175 ml/³/₄ cup sour cream

BUTTERCREAM
1 quantity Basic Vanilla
   Buttercream (see page 20)
a large drop of blue food
   colouring paste

TO DECORATE
48 candy teeth
36 candy eyes
24 jelly beans

muffin pan lined with
* 12 muffin cases*

piping/pastry bag fitted
* with a 'worm' or 'spaghetti'*
* nozzle/tip*

MAKES 12

Preheat the oven to 180°C (350°F) Gas 4.

Sift the flour and baking powder into a bowl, and set aside.

Place the butter and sugar into the bowl of a stand mixer fitted with a paddle attachment (or use a hand-held electric whisk), and beat the mixture at medium to high speed for 1–2 minutes, until light and fluffy. Occasionally stop to scrape down the sides of the bowl with a rubber spatula to make sure that all the butter and sugar is incorporated.

Add the vanilla bean paste and mix. Mixing at low speed, add the eggs, one at a time, beating until incorporated.

Slowly add the sifted dry ingredients, and mix, at low speed, until combined. Scrape down the sides of the bowl with a rubber spatula, and briefly beat at high speed until the mixture is smooth. Add the sour cream and mix until incorporated. Do not over-mix.

Using an ice cream scoop, divide the mixture between the muffin cases, filling to almost two-thirds full. Bake in the preheated oven for 20–25 minutes, until well risen and a skewer inserted into the cakes comes out clean. Transfer to a wire rack to cool completely.

Prepare the Basic Vanilla Buttercream following the instructions on page 20. Add food colouring and fully blend until you have a bright blue.

Spoon the buttercream into the piping/pastry bag. Starting at the outside edge, pipe lines of icing from the edge of the cupcake inwards. Pull the piping/pastry bag away sharply at the end of each line, so that the strings of buttercream snap off from the nozzle/tip and drop down onto the cupcake. Once the first circle is complete, start on another, overlapping your first, but this time starting further away from the edge. Finally, finish the centre by overlapping the second circle. Decorate each monster with four candy teeth, three candy eyes and jelly bean 'horns'.

rainbow swirl cupcake

THESE BRIGHT AND CHEERFUL RAINBOW CUPCAKES WILL BRING A DOSE OF FUN TO YOUNG AND OLD ALIKE. OUR CLASSIC VANILLA CUPCAKE IS TRANSFORMED INTO A RAINBOW BASE AND TOPPED WITH A SWIRL OF MULTI-COLOURED BUTTERCREAM.

200 g self-raising flour/
    1 1/2 cups cake flour mixed
    with 3 teaspoons baking
    powder
1 teaspoon baking powder
175 g/1 1/2 sticks butter
250 g/1 1/4 cups caster/
    granulated sugar
1 1/2 teaspoons vanilla bean
    paste
3 eggs
175 ml/3/4 cup sour cream
1/8 teaspoon each pink, blue
    and yellow food colouring
    pastes (or any other
    colours you like)

BUTTERCREAM
1 quantity Basic Vanilla
    Buttercream (see page 20)
1/8 teaspoon each pink, blue
    and yellow food colouring
    pastes

Preheat the oven to 180°C (350°F) Gas 4.

Sift the flour and baking powder into a bowl and set aside.

Place the butter and sugar into the bowl of a stand mixer fitted with a paddle attachment (or use a hand-held electric whisk), and beat the mixture at medium to high speed for 1–2 minutes, until light and fluffy. Occasionally stop to scrape down the sides of the bowl with a rubber spatula to make sure that all the butter and sugar is incorporated.

Add the vanilla bean paste and mix. Mixing at low speed, add the eggs, one at a time, beating until incorporated.

Slowly add the sifted dry ingredients, and mix, at low speed, until combined. Scrape down the sides of the bowl with a rubber spatula, and briefly beat at high speed until the mixture is smooth. Add the sour cream and mix until incorporated. Do not over-mix.

Now for the fun part! Divide the mixture evenly between 3 bowls, and add one of the food colouring pastes to each bowl. Mix them all thoroughly until well blended.

Take a teaspoonful of one batter and place into each muffin case. Repeat with the other colours, until all the batters have been used up. Now take a cocktail stick/toothpick (or use the end of a knife) and swirl the batters together slightly in a figure of eight.

Feel free to use your own favourite rainbow colours for these cupcakes. Decorate them with brightly coloured sprinkles, or anything that makes you smile.

TO DECORATE
coloured sprinkles

muffin pan lined with 12 muffin cases

piping/pastry bag fitted with a large star nozzle/tip

MAKES 12

Bake in the preheated oven for 20–25 minutes, until well risen and a skewer inserted into the cakes comes out clean. Transfer to a wire rack to cool completely.

Prepare the Basic Vanilla Buttercream following the instructions on page 20.

Using the same technique as for the cake batter, divide the buttercream into three equal portions and colour each portion with one of the three food colouring pastes, mixing until blended.

Spoon one of the buttercreams down one side of the piping/pastry bag leaving space near the nozzle/tip to add the other colours, if possible. Repeat with the second and third colours. You should have a full piping/pastry bag that will allow a little of each colour to be piped onto each cupcake, creating a rainbow effect.

Pipe a swirl of buttercream onto each cupcake, and decorate with coloured sprinkles.

rhubarb and custard cupcake

THIS CUPCAKE WAS INSPIRED BY FOND MEMORIES OF THE RETRO SWEET/CANDY. WITH A SMOOTH, CREAMY CUSTARD AND TART RHUBARB COMPOTE FILLING A VANILLA SPONGE, WE HOPE YOU AGREE THAT OUR REFINED VERSION IS TRULY DELICIOUS.

200 g self-raising flour/1½ cups cake flour mixed with 3 teaspoons baking powder
1 teaspoon baking powder
175 g/1½ sticks butter
250 g/1¼ cups caster/granulated sugar
1½ teaspoons vanilla bean paste
3 eggs
175 ml/¾ cup sour cream

RHUBARB COMPOTE
500 g/1 lb 2 oz. rhubarb, cut into 2.5-cm/1-in. pieces
1 tablespoon orange juice
5 tablespoons caster/granulated sugar

CUSTARD
250 ml/1 cup full-fat/whole milk
3 tablespoons double/heavy cream
1 teaspoon vanilla bean paste

Preheat the oven to 180°C (350°F) Gas 4.

First, make the rhubarb compote. Place the rhubarb into a roasting pan and sprinkle with the orange juice and 4 tablespoons of the sugar. Toss to coat. Cover with foil, then bake in the preheated oven for 20–30 minutes, until the rhubarb is soft but holds its shape. Drain in a sieve/strainer set over a bowl to collect the juice. Reserve 3 tablespoons of the juice and set the rhubarb aside to cool. Leave the oven on. Once cool, reserve 12 pieces of rhubarb for decoration, then mash the rest of the fruit in a bowl with the remaining tablespoon of sugar. Set aside.

To make the custard, place the milk, cream and vanilla bean paste in a saucepan and bring to simmering point over low heat. In a separate bowl, blend the egg yolks, sugar and cornflour/cornstarch. Slowly pour the hot milk onto the eggs, and whisk. Pour the mixture back into the saucepan and heat gently, stirring, until thickened. Pour the custard into a bowl, cover with clingfilm/plastic wrap, and allow to cool.

For the cupcakes, sift the flour and baking powder into a bowl and set aside.

Place the butter and sugar into the bowl of a stand mixer fitted with a paddle attachment (or use a hand-held electric whisk), and beat the mixture at medium to high speed for 1–2 minutes, until light and fluffy.

Add the vanilla bean paste and mix. Mixing at low speed, add the eggs, one at a time, beating until incorporated.

2 egg yolks
1 tablespoon caster/
  granulated sugar
2 teaspoons cornflour/
  cornstarch

BUTTERCREAM
150 g/1¼ sticks butter
1 teaspoon vanilla bean paste
300 g/2½ cups icing/
  confectioners' sugar

*muffin pan lined with
  12 muffin cases*

*piping/pastry bag fitted with
  large star nozzle/tip*

MAKES 12

Slowly add the sifted dry ingredients, and mix on low speed until combined. Scrape down the sides of the bowl with a rubber spatula, and briefly beat at high speed until the mixture is smooth. Add the sour cream and mix until incorporated. Do not over-mix.

Using an ice cream scoop, divide the mixture between the muffin cases, filling to almost two-thirds full. Bake in the preheated oven for 20–25 minutes, until well risen and a skewer inserted into the cakes comes out clean. Transfer to a wire rack to cool completely.

Use a sharp knife or apple corer to remove a small section from the centre of each cupcake. Using a teaspoon (or disposable piping/pastry bags), add some custard followed by some compote. Reserve 1 tablespoon of the custard.

To make the buttercream, place the butter into the bowl of a stand mixer fitted with a paddle attachment (or use a hand-held electric whisk), and beat until soft and fluffy. Add the vanilla bean paste and mix again. Sift in half of the icing/confectioners' sugar and mix at low speed, until incorporated. Add the second half of the sugar, then beat slowly until incorporated. Add the reserved rhubarb juice and custard, beating until light and fluffy.

Spoon the buttercream into the piping/pastry bag, and pipe a swirl of buttercream onto each cupcake. Alternatively, spread the buttercream onto each cake using a palette knife or metal spatula. Top each cupcake with a reserved piece of rhubarb.

jammy dodger cupcake

A TAKE ON ANOTHER CLASSIC BRITISH CHILDHOOD COOKIE. THE VANILLA SPONGE LENDS ITSELF VERY WELL TO A SHARP RASPBERRY FILLING AND VANILLA BUTTERCREAM.

200 g self-raising flour/
    1 1/2 cups cake flour mixed
    with 3 teaspoons baking
    powder
1 teaspoon baking powder
175 g/1 1/2 sticks butter
250 g/1 1/4 cups caster/
    granulated sugar
1 1/2 teaspoons vanilla bean
    paste
3 eggs
175 ml/3/4 cup sour cream

BUTTERCREAM
1 quantity Basic Vanilla
    Buttercream (see page 20)

JAM CORE
175 g/1/2 cup good-quality
    raspberry jam/jelly,
    sieved/strained

TO DECORATE
12 mini jammy dodgers/
    jelly sandwich cookies

muffin pan lined with
    12 muffin cases

piping/pastry bag fitted with
    a large star nozzle/tip

MAKES 12

Preheat the oven to 180°C (350°F) Gas 4.

Sift the flour and baking powder into a bowl and set aside.

Place the butter and sugar into the bowl of a stand mixer fitted with a paddle attachment (or use a hand-held electric whisk), and beat the mixture at medium to high speed for about 1 minute, until light and fluffy. Occasionally stop to scrape down the sides of the bowl with a rubber spatula to make sure that all the butter and sugar is incorporated.

Add the vanilla bean paste and mix. Mixing at low speed, add the eggs, one at a time, beating until incorporated.

Slowly add the sifted dry ingredients, and mix on low speed until combined. Scrape down the sides of the bowl with a rubber spatula, and briefly beat at high speed until the mixture is smooth. Add the sour cream and mix until incorporated. Do not over-mix.

Using an ice cream scoop, divide the mixture between the muffin cases, filling to almost two-thirds full. Bake in the preheated oven for 20–25 minutes, until well risen and a skewer inserted into the cakes comes out clean. Transfer to a wire rack to cool completely.

Prepare the Basic Vanilla Buttercream following the instructions on page 20.

To assemble the cupcakes, use a sharp knife or apple corer to remove a small section from the centre of each cooled cupcake. Using a teaspoon (or disposable piping/pastry bag), fill the holes almost to the top with the sieved/strained raspberry jam/jelly.

Spoon the buttercream into the piping/pastry bag, and pipe a swirl of buttercream onto each cupcake. Alternatively, spread the buttercream onto each cake using a palette knife or metal spatula. Decorate each cupcake with a mini jammy dodger/jelly sandwich cookie.

snowman cupcake

A FUN CUPCAKE TO MAKE YOU SMILE THROUGHOUT THE FESTIVE SEASON. GET THE CHILDREN INVOLVED AND LET YOUR IMAGINATION RUN WILD DECORATING THESE CHEERFUL SNOWMEN. DESICCATED/SHREDDED COCONUT MAKES THE PERFECT SNOW!

200 g self-raising flour/
  1 1/2 cups cake flour mixed
  with 3 teaspoons baking
  powder
1 teaspoon baking powder
175 g/1 1/2 sticks butter
250 g/1 1/4 cups caster/
  granulated sugar
1 1/2 teaspoons vanilla bean
  paste
3 eggs
175 ml/3/4 cup sour cream

BUTTERCREAM
1 quantity Basic Vanilla
  Buttercream (see page 20)

Preheat the oven to 180°C (350°F) Gas 4.

Sift the flour and baking powder into a bowl and set aside.

Place the butter and sugar into the bowl of a stand mixer fitted with a paddle attachment (or use a hand-held electric whisk), and beat the mixture at medium to high speed for 1–2 minutes, until light and fluffy. Occasionally stop to scrape down the sides of the bowl with a rubber spatula to make sure that all the butter and sugar is incorporated.

Add the vanilla bean paste and mix. Mixing at low speed, add the eggs, one at a time, beating until incorporated.

Slowly add the sifted dry ingredients, and mix on low speed until combined. Scrape down the sides of the bowl with a rubber spatula, and briefly beat at high speed until the mixture is smooth. Add the sour cream and mix until incorporated. Do not over-mix.

Using an ice cream scoop, divide the mixture between the muffin cases, filling to almost two-thirds full. Bake in the preheated oven for 20–25 minutes, until well risen and a skewer inserted into the cakes comes out clean. Transfer to a wire rack to cool completely.

Prepare the Basic Vanilla Buttercream following the instructions on page 20.

TO DECORATE

100 g/1 1/8 cups desiccated/
dried unsweetened
shredded coconut
12 white chocolate
confectionery balls
black writing icing
orange writing icing
red strawberry liquorice
laces

*muffin pan lined with
12 muffin cases*

MAKES 12

To decorate your snowmen, spread enough buttercream onto the top of each cupcake to produce a slightly domed effect. We use a cutlery knife to do this. Pour the desiccated/dried unsweetened shredded coconut onto a small plate. Dip the tops of the iced cupcakes into the coconut, so that it sticks to the buttercream, covering it all over. Use your hands to press the coconut onto the buttercream and mould a round surface.

Using a teaspoon, hollow out some of the buttercream to form a dip in the centre of the cupcake buttercream. Place a white chocolate confectionery ball into the dip on each cupcake.

Use black writing icing to draw eyes and a mouth onto each snowman's face. Use the orange writing icing to give each snowman a carrot nose. Take a small piece of strawberry liquorice lace and wrap around the neck of each snowman to create a scarf.

We have used a simple vanilla base here, but feel free to use any flavour base that you love, the effect will be just as fun.

high hat marshmallow cupcake

A LITTLE BIT OF FUN, THESE CUPCAKES USE OUR SENSATIONAL BLACK BOTTOM BASE
AS A FOUNDATION, AND ARE TOPPED WITH FLUFFY HOME-MADE MARSHMALLOW,
THEN DARINGLY DUNKED IN A YUMMY CHOCOLATE COATING.

100 g/3/4 cup plain/
  all-purpose flour
65 g/2/3 cup unsweetened
  cocoa powder
1 teaspoon baking powder
3 eggs
250 g/1 1/4 cups caster/
  granulated sugar
2 tablespoons full-fat/whole
  milk
175 g/1 1/2 sticks butter, melted

MARSHMALLOW
3 egg whites
180 g/1 cup caster/granulated
  sugar
1/4 teaspoon cream of tartar
1/2 teaspoon pure vanilla
  extract

Preheat the oven to 180°C (350°F) Gas 4.

Start by making the marshmallow. Place the egg whites, sugar and
cream of tartar into a heatproof mixing bowl with 2 1/2 tablespoons cold
water. Using a hand-held electric whisk, beat until foamy; this should take
about 1 minute.

Sit the bowl on a small saucepan of simmering water, and beat, using
the electric whisk on a high speed, for 8–10 minutes, until the mixture
hold stiff peaks. Make sure that the water does not touch the bottom
of the bowl. Remove from the heat, then add the vanilla extract and beat
for a further 2 minutes, until thick and glossy. Set aside.

For the cupcakes, sift the flour, cocoa powder and baking powder into
a mixing bowl and set aside.

Place the eggs and sugar into the bowl of a stand mixer fitted with
a whisk attachment (or use a hand-held electric whisk), and beat the
mixture at medium to high speed for about 1 minute, until light and fluffy.

If using a stand mixer, switch to the paddle attachment. Add the sifted
dry ingredients to the batter along with the milk, mixing at low speed to
combine. Add the melted butter and beat until blended. Do not over-mix.

Using an ice cream scoop, divide the mixture between the muffin
cases, filling to almost two-thirds full. Bake in the preheated oven for
20–25 minutes, until well risen and a skewer inserted into the cakes
comes out clean. Transfer to a wire rack to cool completely.

CHOCOLATE COATING

200 g/7 oz. dark/bittersweet chocolate (up to 70% cocoa solids), broken into pieces

150 g/5¹/₂ oz. milk chocolate, broken into pieces

3 tablespoons vegetable oil

muffin pan lined with 12 muffin cases

piping/pastry bag fitted with a large round nozzle/tip

MAKES 12

To make the chocolate coating, place the two different chocolates into a heatproof bowl with the oil. Set the bowl over a saucepan of simmering water, and allow to melt slowly, stirring until smooth and glossy. Make sure that the water does not touch the bottom of the bowl. Pour into a small deep bowl and allow to cool for 15 minutes.

To assemble the cakes, spoon the marshmallow into the piping bag, and pipe a spiral of marshmallow onto each cooled cupcake, trying to make a small peak when you lift the nozzle off.

Holding each cake by the base, quickly dip the marshmallow into the chocolate coating, using a twisting motion to lift the cupcake out of the chocolate. Do not linger in the chocolate, as the marshmallow can slide off the base! This technique can be tricky, but remember you can fill in any white gaps with a drizzle of the chocolate coating. Place on a wire rack and allow any excess coating to drip off, then leave to set in the refrigerator. Bring to room temperature to serve.

DIVINE DESSERTS

PLUM BAKEWELL CUPCAKE

APPLE CRUMBLE CUPCAKE

STICKY TOFFEE PUDDING CUPCAKE

RASPBERRY PAVLOVA CUPCAKE

MERINGUE CUPCAKE

BANOFFEE CUPCAKE

STRAWBERRIES AND CREAM CUPCAKE

RASPBERRY CHEESECAKE CUPCAKE

plum bakewell cupcake

AT LOLA'S WE WANTED TO CREATE SOMETHING A LITTLE DIFFERENT FROM THE CLASSIC BAKEWELL TART, BUT SOMETHING THAT YOU WILL REMEMBER JUST AS FONDLY. THIS CUPCAKE IS A DELIGHTFUL TWIST ON THE CLASSIC RASPBERRY AND ALMOND FLAVOURS. A MOIST ALMOND SPONGE HIDES A TART PLUM COMPOTE. EVERYTHING IS TOPPED OFF WITH A BUTTERY ALMOND BUTTERCREAM AND A DRIZZLE OF COMPOTE. DELICIOUS!

125 g/1 1/8 sticks butter
200 g/1 cup caster/granulated sugar
1 teaspoon almond extract
3 eggs
3/4 teaspoon baking powder
175 g self-raising flour/1 1/3 cups cake flour mixed with 2 teaspoons baking powder
125 ml/1/2 cup sour cream

PLUM COMPOTE
250 g/1/2 lb. plums
75 g/1/2 cup soft light brown sugar
2 tablespoons orange juice

Preheat the oven to 180°C (350°F) Gas 4.

Place the butter, sugar and almond extract into the bowl of a stand mixer fitted with a paddle attachment (or use a hand-held electric whisk), and beat the mixture at medium to high speed for 1–2 minutes, until light and fluffy.

Add the eggs, one at a time, mixing at low speed, until fully incorporated. Scrape down the sides of the bowl with a rubber spatula to make sure all the mixture is fully incorporated.

In another bowl, sift together the flour and baking powder, and add to the butter mixture, a little at a time, mixing at low speed until smooth. Finally add the sour cream and beat briefly until fully blended.

Using an ice cream scoop, divide the mixture between the muffin cases, filling to almost two-thirds full. Bake in the preheated oven for 20 minutes, until well risen and a skewer inserted into a cakes comes out clean. Transfer to a wire rack to cool completely.

Halve the plums, remove the stones/pits and slice the flesh. Place the sliced plums in a saucepan, add the sugar and orange juice, and gently simmer over medium to low heat until the fruit is a jammy consistency (this will take about 20 minutes). Set aside to cool.

BUTTERCREAM
150 g/1¼ sticks butter
½ teaspoon almond extract
300 g/2½ cups icing/
   confectioners' sugar
3–4 tablespoons full-fat/
   whole milk

TO DECORATE
toasted flaked/sliced almonds

*muffin pan lined with
   12 muffin cases*

*piping/pastry bag fitted with
   a large star nozzle/tip*

MAKES 12

To make the buttercream, place the butter into the bowl of a stand mixer fitted with a paddle attachment (or use a hand-held electric whisk), and beat until soft and fluffy. Add the almond extract and mix. Sift in half the icing/confectioners' sugar, mixing slowly until smooth. Add the second half of the icing/confectioners' sugar, mixing at low speed, until incorporated. Finally add most of the milk and beat until light and fluffy. If the icing is too stiff add a little more milk.

To assemble the cupcakes, use a sharp knife or apple corer to remove a small section from the centre of each cupcake. Set aside a little of the cooled compote for decorating, then using a teaspoon (or disposable piping/pastry bag), fill the holes almost to the top with the compote.

Spoon the buttercream into the piping/pastry bag, and pipe a swirl onto each cake. Alternatively, spread the buttercream onto each cupcake using a palette knife or metal spatula.

Decorate each cake with the toasted flaked/sliced almonds and a drizzle of the reserved compote.

We think the plum compote is a nice twist on the classic bakewell flavours, however you could always make a raspberry or cherry compote if you prefer.

apple crumble cupcake

CREATED FOR LOLA'S 'BEST OF BRITISH' RANGE, THIS APPLE CRUMBLE CUPCAKE IS EVERYTHING WE LOVE IN THE CLASSIC DESSERT CAPTURED IN A CAKE. A WARMING CINNAMON AND APPLE CAKE IS COVERED IN A CINNAMON CREAM CHEESE ICING AND FINISHED OFF WITH A BUTTERY CRUMBLE TOPPING.

175 g self-raising flour/1 1/3 cups cake flour mixed with 2 teaspoons baking powder
1 1/2 teaspoons ground cinnamon
3/4 teaspoon baking powder
125 g/1 1/8 sticks unsalted butter
200 g/1 cup soft light brown sugar
1/2 teaspoon vanilla bean paste
3 eggs
2 tablespoons sour cream
2 Granny Smith apples, peeled and very finely chopped

Preheat the oven to 180°C (350°F) Gas 4.

Start by making the crumble topping. Place the flour, almonds and sugar into a bowl. Using your fingertips, rub the cold butter into the dry ingredients, until it resembles breadcrumbs. Spread the crumble mix onto the lined baking sheet and bake in the preheated oven for 15 minutes, turning the mixture with a spatula every 5 minutes to ensure the crumbs are baked evenly. Once golden brown, remove from the oven to cool. Leave the oven on for the cupcakes. The crumble mixture will keep in an airtight container for up to 10 days.

For the cupcakes, sift the flour, cinnamon and baking powder into a mixing bowl, and set aside.

Place the butter, sugar and vanilla bean paste into the bowl of a stand mixer fitted with a paddle attachment (or use a hand-held electric whisk), and beat the mixture at medium to high speed for 1–2 minutes, until light and fluffy.

Add the eggs, one at a time, beating at low speed, until fully incorporated.

Slowly add the sifted dry ingredients, and mix on low speed until combined. Scrape down the sides of the bowl with a rubber spatula, and briefly beat at high speed until the mixture is smooth. Add the sour cream and mix until incorporated. Do not over-mix. Stir in the apples.

CRUMBLE TOPPING
125 g/1 cup minus
  1 tablespoon plain/
  all-purpose flour
25 g/¼ cup ground almonds
50 g/¼ cup caster/granulated
  sugar
110 g/1 stick cold butter,
  cubed

CREAM CHEESE ICING
1 quantity Basic Cream
  Cheese Icing (see page 21)
1 teaspoon ground cinnamon

*large baking sheet lined
  with baking parchment*

*muffin pan lined with
  12 muffin cases*

*piping/pastry bag fitted
  with a large star nozzle/tip
  (optional)*

MAKES 12

Using an ice cream scoop, divide the mixture between the muffin cases, filling to almost two-thirds full. Bake in the preheated oven for 20–25 minutes, until well risen and a skewer inserted into a cakes comes out clean. Transfer to a wire rack and to cool completely.

Prepare the Basic Cream Cheese Icing following the instructions on page 21, adding the cinnamon with the vanilla bean paste.

Spread the cream cheese icing onto the cooled cupcakes using a palette knife or metal spatula. Alternatively, spoon it into a piping/pastry bag fitted with a large star nozzle/tip and pipe a swirl onto the top of each cupcake.

Decorate each cake with a small sprinkle of the baked crumble mixture, and then sit back and enjoy!

A fruity crumble cupcake is the perfect Sunday afternoon treat! Instead of apples you could try pears, both work well with the cinnamon cream cheese icing and buttery crumble topping.

sticky toffee pudding cupcake

LOLA'S STICKY TOFFEE CUPCAKE IS PERFECT SERVED WITH VANILLA ICE CREAM.

180 g/1 cup chopped dates
150 ml/²/₃ cup boiling water
180 g self-raising flour/1¹/₃
   cups cake flour mixed with
   2 teaspoons baking powder
1 teaspoon bicarbonate
   of soda/baking soda
100 g/1 stick minus
   1 tablespoon butter
150 g/³/₄ cup dark muscovado
   sugar
1 teaspoon vanilla bean paste
2 eggs

BUTTERCREAM
125 g/1¹/₈ sticks butter
1 teaspoon vanilla bean paste
350 g/3 cups icing/
   confectioners' sugar
1 tablespoon full-fat/whole milk
150 g/¹/₂ cup store-bought
   caramel

TO DECORATE
25 g/¹/₄ cup chopped dates

muffin pan lined with
   12 muffin cases

piping/pastry bag fitted with
   a large star nozzle/tip

MAKES 12

Preheat the oven to 180°C (350°F) Gas 4.

Leave the chopped dates to soak in boiling water for 20 minutes.

Sift the flour and bicarbonate of soda/baking soda into a bowl and set aside.

Place the butter, sugar and vanilla bean paste into the bowl of a stand mixer fitted with a paddle attachment (or use a hand-held electric whisk) and beat at medium to high speed for 1–2 minutes, until light and fluffy. Scrape down the sides of the bowl with a rubber spatula, to incorporate all the butter and sugar into the mixture.

Add the eggs, one at a time, mixing at low speed, until incorporated.

Slowly add the sifted dry ingredients, and mix at low speed until combined. Scrape down the sides of the bowl with a rubber spatula, and briefly beat at high speed until the mixture is smooth.

Mash the soaked dates with a fork, then fold into the batter to combine.

Using an ice cream scoop, divide the mixture between the muffin cases, filling to almost two-thirds full. Bake in the preheated oven for 18–20 minutes, until well risen and a skewer inserted into the cakes comes out clean. Transfer to a wire rack to cool completely.

To make the buttercream, place the butter into the bowl of a stand mixer fitted with a paddle attachment (or use a hand-held electric whisk) and beat until soft and fluffy. Add the vanilla bean paste and mix again, until combined. Sift in half of the icing/confectioners' sugar and mix at low speed until incorporated. Add the second half of the sugar, then beat slowly until all the sugar is incorporated. Add the milk and beat until light and fluffy. Finally, mix in the caramel. If the icing is too stiff, add a little more milk.

Spoon the buttercream into the piping/pastry bag, and pipe a swirl of buttercream onto each cupcake. Alternatively, spread the buttercream onto each cake using a palette knife or metal spatula. Decorate with chopped dates.

raspberry pavlova cupcake

THIS IS A DELICIOUS REMINDER OF SUNSHINE AND ALL THINGS SUMMERY. OUR SLIGHTLY SHARP RASPBERRY SPONGE HIDES A FRUITY RASPBERRY COMPOTE AND IS TOPPED WITH A DELICIOUS CHANTILLY CREAM, CRISP CRUMBLED MERINGUE AND A FRESH RASPBERRY.

180 g/1⅓ cups plain/
   all-purpose flour
1½ teaspoons baking powder
180 g/1½ sticks butter
180 g/1 cup minus 1½
   tablespoons caster/
   granulated sugar
1 teaspoon vanilla bean paste
3 eggs
120 g/¾ cup fresh raspberries

RASPBERRY COMPOTE
150 g/1 cup fresh raspberries
1½ tablespoons raspberry
   jam/jelly

CHANTILLY CREAM
400 ml/1¾ cups double/
   heavy cream
1 teaspoon icing/
   confectioners' sugar sifted
1 teaspoon vanilla bean paste

TO DECORATE
3 individual store-bought
   meringue nests
12 fresh raspberries

*muffin pan lined with
   12 muffin cases*

*piping/pastry bag fitted with
   a large round nozzle/tip*

MAKES 12

Preheat the oven to 180°C (350°F) Gas 4.

Sift the flour and baking powder into a bowl, and set aside.

Place the butter and sugar into the bowl of a stand mixer fitted with a paddle attachment (or use a hand-held electric whisk), and beat the mixture at medium to high speed for 1–2 minutes, until light and fluffy. Occasionally stop to scrape down the sides of the bowl with a rubber spatula to make sure that all the butter and sugar is incorporated.

Add the vanilla bean paste and mix. Add the eggs, one at a time, mixing at low speed, until fully incorporated.

Slowly add the sifted dry ingredients, mixing at low speed, until combined. Add the fresh raspberries and beat briefly at medium speed to slightly break up the raspberries and incorporate them into the batter.

Using an ice cream scoop, divide the mixture between the muffin cases, filling to almost two-thirds full. Bake in the preheated oven for 20–25 minutes, until well risen and a skewer inserted into the cakes comes out clean. Transfer to a wire rack to cool completely.

For the compote, place the raspberries and jam/jelly into a mixing bowl and mash with a fork until you have slightly lumpy compote. Do not break down the raspberries too much as you still want some texture.

To assemble the cupcakes, use a sharp knife or apple corer to remove a small section from the centre of each cupcake. Using a teaspoon (or disposable piping/pastry bag), fill the holes almost to the top with compote.

Crumble the meringues into small pieces and set aside.

To make the Chantilly cream, place all the ingredients into a large mixing bowl and, using a hand-held electric whisk, beat until soft peaks form and the cream holds its shape; this will take about 2 minutes. This can also be done by hand with a balloon whisk.

Spoon the Chantilly cream into the piping/pastry bag and pipe a swirl onto the top of each filled cupcake. Alternatively, spread the Chantilly cream onto each cake using a palette knife or metal spatula.

Decorate each cupcake with crumbled meringue and a raspberry.

meringue cupcake

BASED AROUND THE IDEA OF A LEMON MERINGUE PIE, A ZINGY LEMON SPONGE HIDES A FRESH RASPBERRY COMPOTE AND IS TOPPED WITH MARSHMALLOWY MERINGUE. IF YOU HAVE A COOK'S MINI BLOWTORCH YOU CAN FINISH THE CUPCAKE WITH A FANCY TOASTED TEXTURE. IF YOU DON'T HAVE ONE IT WILL STILL TASTE DIVINE!

225 g self-raising flour/1³/₄ cups cake flour mixed with 4 teaspoons baking powder
¹/₂ teaspoon baking powder
175 g/³/₄ cup plus 2 tablespoons caster/granulated sugar
grated zest from 2 lemons
3 eggs
50 g/¹/₄ cup lemon curd
75 ml/¹/₃ cup sour cream
175 g/1¹/₂ sticks butter, melted

RASPBERRY COMPOTE
150 g/1 cup fresh raspberries
1¹/₂ tablespoons raspberry jam/jelly

Preheat the oven to 180°C (350°F) Gas 4.

Sift the flour and baking powder into a large mixing bowl, then add the sugar and lemon zest and set aside.

Into another bowl, place the eggs, lemon curd and sour cream, and whisk with a balloon whisk, until fully combined. Pour this into the flour mixture and add the melted butter. Mix until smooth and all ingredients are fully incorporated.

Using an ice cream scoop, divide the mixture between the muffin cases, filling to almost two-thirds full. Bake in the preheated oven for 20–25 minutes, until well risen and a skewer inserted into the cakes comes out clean. Transfer to a wire rack to cool completely.

For the compote, place the raspberries and jam/jelly into a mixing bowl and mash with a fork, until you have a slightly lumpy compote. Do not break down the raspberries too much as you still want some texture.

MERINGUE

3 egg whites

180 g/1 cup minus 1½ tablespoons caster/ granulated sugar

¼ teaspoon cream of tartar

½ teaspoon pure vanilla extract

muffin pan lined with 12 muffin cases

piping/pastry bag fitted with a small star nozzle/tip

cook's blowtorch (optional)

MAKES 12

To make the meringue, place the egg whites, sugar, cream of tartar and 3 tablespoons water into a heatproof mixing bowl and, using an electric whisk, beat for about a minute until foamy. Bring a small saucepan of water to a simmer and set the bowl on top of the pan, making sure that the water does not touch the bottom of the bowl. Beat the mixture at a high speed for approximately 8 minutes. The mixture will thicken slowly, and when it forms peaks that hold their shape, remove the bowl from the heat and add the vanilla extract. Beat for 2 minutes more, until it is thick and holds its shape. Set aside.

To assemble the cupcakes, use a sharp knife or apple corer to remove a small section from the centre of each cupcake. Using a teaspoon (or disposable piping/pastry bag), fill the holes almost to the top with the compote.

To decorate, spoon the meringue into the piping/pastry bag, and pipe small teardrops around the edge of the cake, pulling away quickly to achieve a peak effect. Continue until the surface of each cake is covered.

Serve as they are, or wave a cook's blowtorch across the tops to caramelize the meringue, giving it a lovely tarnished tone and delicious toasted texture.

banoffee cupcake

FANS OF LOLA'S BANANA CUPCAKES WILL LOVE THIS BANOFFEE VARIATION. THE DELICIOUS FEATURES OF THE ORIGINAL BANANA CAKE COMBINE WITH RICH GOOEY CARAMEL AND A CREAMY MASCARPONE ICING, TOPPED WITH YET MORE CARAMEL AND CHOCOLATE CURLS. NOT ONE FOR A DIET DAY BUT A REAL TREAT NONETHELESS.

225 g/1¾ cups plain/
   all-purpose flour
1 teaspoon baking powder
½ teaspoon bicarbonate of
   soda/baking soda
110 g/1 stick butter, melted
170 g/¾ cup caster/
   granulated sugar
1 teaspoon vanilla bean paste
2 eggs
3 medium ripe bananas,
   mashed
120 g/⅓ cup store-bought
   caramel

MASCARPONE ICING
200 g/7 oz. mascarpone
   cheese
110 g/4 oz. full-fat cream
   cheese
1 teaspoon vanilla bean paste
125 g/1 cup icing/
   confectioners' sugar

Preheat the oven to 180°C (350°F) Gas 4.

Sift the flour, baking powder and bicarbonate of soda/baking soda into a bowl, and set aside.

Place the butter and sugar into the bowl of a stand mixer fitted with a paddle attachment (or use a hand-held electric whisk), and beat the mixture at medium to high speed for 1–2 minutes, until light and fluffy. Occasionally stop to scrape down the sides of the bowl with a rubber spatula to make sure that all the butter and sugar is incorporated.

Add the vanilla bean paste and mix. Then, at low speed, add the eggs, one at a time, until fully incorporated.

Add the mashed bananas and combine. Slowly add the sifted dry ingredients, and mix at low speed until combined. Scrape down the sides of the bowl with a rubber spatula, and briefly beat at high speed until the mixture is smooth. Do not over-mix.

Using an ice cream scoop, divide the mixture between the muffin cases, filling to almost two-thirds full. To give each cupcake a gooey caramel centre once baked, place the caramel into a disposable piping/pastry bag, and divide it evenly among the muffin cases, carefully inserting the nozzle/tip about halfway into each muffin case of batter. Alternatively, half-fill each cupcake case with batter, add some caramel, then top with the remaining batter.

divine desserts 131

TO DECORATE

1 ripe banana sliced into 12 pieces
50 g/⅛ cup store-bought caramel
chocolate curls (optional)

muffin pan lined with 12 muffin cases

piping/pastry bag fitted with a small round nozzle/tip (optional)

piping/pastry bag fitted with a large star nozzle/tip

MAKES 12

Bake in the preheated oven for 25 minutes, until well risen and a skewer inserted into the cakes comes out clean. Transfer to a wire rack to cool completely.

Place the mascarpone and cream cheese into the bowl of a stand mixer fitted with a paddle attachment (or use a hand-held electric whisk) and beat slowly until smooth and combined. Add the vanilla bean paste and mix to combine. Sift in half of the icing/confectioners' sugar and, mixing at low speed, mix until incorporated. Add the second half of the sugar, then beat slowly until all the sugar is incorporated.

Spoon the icing into the piping/pastry bag, and pipe a swirl of icing onto each cupcake. Alternatively, spread the icing onto each cake using a palette knife or metal spatula.

To decorate, place a slice of fresh banana in the middle of each cake and drizzle with a small amount of caramel. Finish with a sprinkle of chocolate curls, if you like.

strawberries and cream cupcake

NOTHING SUMS UP A BRITISH SUMMER LIKE STRAWBERRIES AND CREAM! HERE, OUR VANILLA-SCENTED CUPCAKE BASE HOLDS A DELICIOUS FRESH STRAWBERRY COMPOTE AND IS TOPPED OFF WITH A HEAVENLY CLOUD OF STRAWBERRY WHIPPED CREAM.

200 g self-raising flour/1½
    cups cake flour mixed with
    3 teaspoons baking powder
1 teaspoon baking powder
175 g/1½ sticks butter
250 g/1¼ cups caster/
    granulated sugar
1½ teaspoons vanilla bean
    paste
3 eggs
175 ml/¾ cup sour cream

STRAWBERRY COMPOTE
16 fresh strawberries, finely
    chopped
5 tablespoons caster/
    granulated sugar
4 teaspoons freshly squeezed
    lemon juice
2 tablespoons cornflour/
    cornstarch, sifted

Preheat the oven to 180°C (350°F) Gas 4.

Sift the flour and baking powder into a bowl and set aside.

Place the butter and sugar into the bowl of a stand mixer fitted with a paddle attachment (or use a hand-held electric whisk), and beat the mixture at medium to high speed for 1–2 minutes, until light and fluffy. Occasionally stop to scrape down the sides of the bowl with a rubber spatula to make sure that all the butter and sugar is incorporated.

Add the vanilla bean paste and mix. Mixing at low speed, add the eggs, one at a time, beating until incorporated.

Slowly add the sifted dry ingredients, and mix at low speed until combined. Scrape down the sides of the bowl with a rubber spatula, and briefly beat at high speed until the mixture is smooth. Add the sour cream and mix until incorporated. Do not over-mix.

Using an ice cream scoop, divide the mixture between the muffin cases, filling to almost two-thirds full. Bake in the preheated oven for 20–25 minutes, until well risen and a skewer inserted into the cakes comes out clean. Transfer to a wire rack to cool completely.

Meanwhile, make the strawberry compote. Place the chopped strawberries, sugar and lemon juice into a small saucepan set over medium heat. Stir constantly for about 3 minutes or until the strawberries start to give up their juice and soften. Simmer for 2 minutes more then add the cornflour/cornstarch. Stir to mix and allow it to bubble for a minute or so to cook the cornflour/cornstarch.

CREAM TOPPING
400 ml/1¾ cups double/
    heavy cream
½ teaspoon vanilla bean paste

TO DECORATE
3–4 fresh strawberries

*muffin pan lined with
    12 muffin cases*

*piping/pastry bag fitted with
    a large round nozzle/tip*

MAKES 12

The mixture should be quite thick but with pieces of strawberry suspended in the gel. Set aside to cool until needed.

To assemble the cupcakes, use a sharp knife or apple corer to remove a small section from the centre of each cupcake. Reserve 2 tablespoons of the compote for the topping, then, using a teaspoon (or disposable piping/pastry bag), fill the holes almost to the top with compote.

To decorate, place the double/heavy cream and vanilla bean paste into a large mixing bowl and, using a hand-held electric whisk, beat at medium speed, until thickened but not forming peaks. Add the reserved strawberry compote and whisk at low speed until soft peaks form and the cream holds its shape.

Spoon the cream topping into the piping/pastry bag, and pipe a swirl onto each cupcake. Finish with a slice of fresh strawberry. Store in the refrigerator, if not eating immediately. They will keep for 2 days.

*These cupcakes are perfect for serving at a garden
party on a warm summer's day, along with
a glass of something chilled and bubbly.*

raspberry cheesecake cupcake

BASE
140 g/5 oz. digestive biscuits/graham crackers, crushed

20 g/⅛ cup finely chopped white chocolate

60 g/½ stick butter, melted

FILLING
500 g/1 lb. 2 oz. full-fat cream cheese

30 g/scant 3½ tablespoons plain/all-purpose flour, sifted

150 g/¾ cup caster/granulated sugar

2 eggs

1½ teaspoons vanilla bean paste

75 ml/⅓ cup sour cream

36 fresh raspberries

TO DECORATE
50 ml/¼ cup double/heavy cream, lightly whipped

12 fresh raspberries

1 tablespoon crumb base mixture (reserved from recipe)

muffin pan lined with 12 muffin cases

MAKES 12

WE THINK THAT EVERYTHING TASTES BETTER IN INDIVIDUAL PORTIONS, SO HAVE CREATED THESE RASPBERRY CHEESECAKE 'CUPCAKES'. A LITTLE HIDDEN TREAT OF WHITE CHOCOLATE IS CONCEALED WITHIN THE BUTTERY BISCUIT BASE.

Preheat the oven to 180°C (350°F) Gas 4.

In a mixing bowl, mix together the biscuit/cracker crumbs, chocolate and melted butter to a sandy consistency. Reserve a tablespoon for decoration, then divide the remaining mixture among the muffin cases, pressing down firmly.

Place the cream cheese into the bowl of a stand mixer fitted with a paddle attachment (or use a hand-held electric whisk) and beat until smooth, then add the flour, sugar, eggs, vanilla and sour cream, beating at low speed until the mixture is smooth, light and fluffy.

Place 3 raspberries on top of the crumbs in each case, then top with the cheese mixture, until each case is almost full. Bake in the preheated oven for 20–25 minutes or until the filling is set, but still slightly wobbly in the centre. Set aside to cool for 30 minutes, before removing from the muffin pan and allowing to fully cool in the refrigerator for at least an hour, or ideally overnight.

To serve, top each cake with a spoonful of whipped cream and a raspberry. Sprinkle the remaining crumbs in a small line across the top of each cake to finish. Store in the refrigerator, but remove at least 30 minutes before eating to enjoy them at their best.

COCKTAIL HOUR

MOJITO CUPCAKE

COSMOPOLITAN CUPCAKE

LYCHEE MARTINI CUPCAKE

CHOCOLATE GUINNESS CUPCAKE

PINA COLADA CUPCAKE

CHAMPAGNE CUPCAKE

mojito cupcake

THIS ZESTY MOJITO CUPCAKE HAS A FRESH MINTY KICK.

175 g self-raising flour/1 1/3 cups cake flour mixed with 2 teaspoons baking powder
3/4 teaspoon baking powder
125 g/1 1/8 sticks butter
100 g/1/2 cup caster/superfine sugar
100 g/1/2 cup soft light brown sugar
1 teaspoon vanilla bean paste
3 eggs
125 g/1/3 cup sour cream
2 teaspoons chopped mint
freshly squeezed juice of 1 lime
grated zest from 2 limes

KIWI MINT CORE
3 kiwi fruits, peeled and chopped
1 teaspoon chopped mint

MASCARPONE ICING
150 g/1 1/4 sticks butter
250 g/1 cup mascarpone
150 g/1 1/4 cups icing/confectioners' sugar, sifted
40 g/1/4 cup lime curd
2 teaspoons freshly squeezed lime juice
grated zest from 2 limes

TO DECORATE
mint leaves
grated lime zest

muffin pan lined with 12 muffin cases

piping/pastry bag fitted with a large star nozzle/tip

MAKES 12

Preheat the oven to 180°C (350°F) Gas 4.

Sift the flour and baking powder into a bowl and set aside.

Place the butter and both types of sugar into the bowl of a stand mixer fitted with a paddle attachment (or use a hand-held electric whisk), and beat at medium to high speed for 1–2 minutes, until light and fluffy. Occasionally stop to scrape down the sides of the bowl with a rubber spatula to make sure that all the butter and sugar is incorporated.

Add the vanilla bean paste and mix, then, add the eggs, one at a time, beating on low speed until incorporated.

Slowly add the sifted dry ingredients, and mix on low speed until combined. Scrape down the sides of the bowl with a rubber spatula, and briefly beat at high speed until the mixture is smooth. Add the sour cream, lime juice and zest, and mix until incorporated. Do not over-mix.

Using an ice cream scoop, divide the mixture between the muffin cases, filling to almost two-thirds full. Bake in the preheated oven for 20–25 minutes, until well risen and a skewer inserted into the cakes comes out clean. Transfer to a wire rack to cool completely.

To make the kiwi mint core, blend the kiwi fruits and mint in a food processor until smooth. Set aside.

For the mascarpone icing, place the ingredients into the bowl of a stand mixer fitted with a paddle attachment (or use a hand-held electric whisk). Beat for 1 minute on medium speed then beat on high until very smooth.

To assemble the cupcakes, use a sharp knife or apple corer to remove a small section from the centre of each cupcake. Using a teaspoon (or disposable piping/pastry bag), fill the holes almost to the top with the kiwi mint filling.

Spoon the icing into the piping/pastry bag and pipe a swirl onto each cupcake. Alternatively, spread the icing onto each cake using a palette knife or metal spatula. Decorate with mint leaves and lime zest.

cosmopolitan cupcake

A GLAMOROUS GROWN UP TREAT –
THIS ONE IS NOT FOR CHILDREN!

200 g/1 1/2 cups plain/
  all-purpose flour
1 teaspoon baking powder
90 g/3/4 stick butter
190 g/scant 1 cup caster/
  superfine sugar
3 eggs
100 ml/1/2 cup full-fat/whole
  milk
3 tablespoons freshly
  squeezed lime juice
grated zest from 1 lime

GRAND MARNIER SYRUP
2 tablespoons freshly
  squeezed orange juice
50 g/1/4 cup caster/superfine
  sugar
2 tablespoons Grand Marnier

BUTTERCREAM
150 g/1 1/4 sticks butter
400 g/2 3/4 cups icing/
  confectioners' sugar
1 teaspoon vanilla bean paste
1 tablespoon vodka
4 tablespoons pomegranate
  molasses
1/2 teaspoon pink food
  colouring paste

TO DECORATE
12 lime slices

*muffin pan lined with
12 muffin cases*

*piping/pastry bag fitted with
a large star nozzle/tip*

MAKES 12

Preheat the oven to 180°C (350°F) Gas 4.

Start by making the Grand Marnier syrup. Place the orange juice, sugar and Grand Marnier in a saucepan and heat gently until the sugar has dissolved. Take off the heat and leave to cool slightly.

Sift the flour and baking powder into a bowl and set aside.

Place the butter and sugar into the bowl of a stand mixer fitted with a paddle attachment (or use a hand-held electric whisk), and beat the mixture at medium to high speed for 1–2 minutes, until light and fluffy. Occasionally stop to scrape down the sides of the bowl with a rubber spatula to make sure that all the butter and sugar is incorporated. Add the eggs, one at a time, until fully incorporated.

Mix the milk, lime juice and zest together – don't worry it will curdle! Gradually add this to the butter and egg mixture, alternating with the sifted flour mixture, until you have a smooth batter and all the ingredients have been incorporated. Using an ice cream scoop, divide the mixture between the muffin cases, filling to almost two-thirds full.

Bake in the preheated oven for 20–25 minutes, until well risen and a skewer inserted into the cakes comes out clean. Transfer to a wire rack and allow to cool for 15 minutes, then brush generously with the Grand Marnier syrup.

To make the buttercream, place the butter into the bowl of a stand mixer fitted with a paddle attachment (or use a hand-held electric whisk), and beat until soft and fluffy. Sift in half of the icing/confectioners' sugar and, with the mixer on low speed, mix until incorporated. Add the second half of the sugar, along with the vanilla bean paste, vodka, pomegranate molasses and food colouring paste, then beat, slowly, until smooth. This will take 1–2 minutes. Scrape the sides of the bowl down and give the buttercream a final beat until light and fluffy.

Spoon the buttercream into the piping/pastry bag, and pipe a swirl of buttercream onto each cupcake. Alternatively, spread the buttercream onto each cake using a palette knife or metal spatula. Decorate each cupcake with a slice of lime.

lychee martini cupcake

FRAGRANT AND FRUITY JUST LIKE THE DELICIOUS COCKTAIL, THESE LYCHEE CUPCAKES ARE SOAKED WITH AN ALCOHOLIC SYRUP, MAKING THEM VERY MOIST AND TASTY.

175 g/1 1/3 cups plain/
  all-purpose flour
1 teaspoon baking powder
175 g/1 1/2 sticks butter
175 g/3/4 cup plus
  2 tablespoons caster/
  superfine sugar
3 eggs
2 tablespoons freshly
  squeezed lychee juice
100 g/3 1/2 oz. lychees, peeled
  and quartered

LYCHEE VODKA SYRUP
100 ml/1/3 cup freshly
  squeezed lychee juice
2 tablespoons vodka

COMPOTE
150 g/1 cup raspberries
1/4 teaspoon rose water
3 tablespoons raspberry
  jam/jelly
1 tablespoon freshly squeezed
  lychee juice
1 teaspoon icing/
  confectioners' sugar

Preheat the oven to 180°C (350°F) Gas 4.

First, make the lychee vodka syrup, by mixing the lychee juice and vodka together in a small bowl. Set aside.

Sift the flour and baking powder into a mixing bowl and set aside.

Place the butter and sugar into the bowl of a stand mixer fitted with a paddle attachment (or use a hand-held electric whisk), and beat the mixture at medium to high speed for 1–2 minutes, until light and fluffy. Occasionally stop to scrape down the sides of the bowl with a rubber spatula to make sure that all the butter and sugar is incorporated.

Add the eggs, one at a time, mixing on low speed, until fully incorporated. Add the sifted dry ingredients, and mix on low speed until combined. Add the lychee juice, mixing slowly, until the batter is smooth. Stir in the lychee pieces.

Using an ice cream scoop, divide the mixture between the muffin cases, filling to almost two-thirds full. Bake in the preheated oven for 22–25 minutes, until well risen and a skewer inserted into the cake comes out clean. Transfer to a wire rack and immediately brush with the lychee vodka syrup. Divide the syrup evenly between the cakes until you have used it all up. Transfer to a wire rack to cool completely.

For the compote, place all the ingredients into a bowl and mash with a fork until you have a combination of smooth purée and textured pieces of raspberry. Set aside.

To make the buttercream, place the butter into a stand mixer fitted with a paddle attachment (or use a hand-held electric whisk) and beat

BUTTERCREAM
150 g/1 1/4 sticks butter
250 g/2 cups icing/
   confectioners' sugar
1 tablespoon lychee juice
1 1/2 teaspoons pomegranate
   molasses
pink food colouring paste

TO DECORATE
6 lychees, halved
12 raspberries
edible sugar pearls

*muffin pan lined with
   12 muffin cases*

*piping/pastry bag fitted with
   a large star nozzle/tip*

MAKES 12

until soft and fluffy. Sift in half of the icing/confectioners' sugar and mix at low speed, until incorporated. Add the second half of the sugar, then beat, slowly, until incorporated. Add the lychee juice and pomegranate molasses and mix until combined. Using the tip of a sharp knife, take a very small amount of pink food colouring paste, and add it to the buttercream. Blend until the colour is your desired shade of pink but do not over-mix.

To assemble the cupcakes, use a sharp knife or apple corer to remove a small section from the centre of each cupcake. Using a teaspoon (or disposable piping/pastry bag), fill the holes almost to the top with compote.

Spoon the buttercream into the piping/pastry bag and pipe a swirl onto each cupcake. Alternatively, spread the buttercream onto each cake using a palette knife or metal spatula. Decorate with lychee halves, raspberries and sugar pearls.

Our aim was to capture the delicate nature of this cocktail and transform it into a delightful teatime treat.

chocolate guinness cupcake

A NEW ADDITION TO LOLA'S, THIS IS A DECADENT TREAT. DENSE CHOCOLATE
SPONGE IS TOPPED OFF WITH A COOL CREAM CHEESE ICING THAT RESEMBLES
THE COLOURS OF A PINT OF STOUT. A 'GROWN UP' CHOCOLATE CUPCAKE.

200 g/1 1/2 cups plain/
   all-purpose flour
1 1/2 teaspoons bicarbonate of
   soda/baking soda
175 ml/3/4 cup Guinness
175 g/1 1/2 sticks butter
50 g/1/2 cup unsweetened
   cocoa powder
250 g/1 1/4 cups caster/
   granulated sugar
1 egg
100 ml/1/3 cup sour cream
1 teaspoon vanilla bean paste

CREAM CHEESE ICING
1 quantity Basic Cream
   Cheese Icing (see page 21)

TO DECORATE
dark/bittersweet chocolate
   shavings

muffin pan lined with
   12 muffin cases

piping/pastry bag fitted with
   a large round nozzle/tip

MAKES 12

Preheat the oven to 180°C (350°F) Gas 4.

Sift the flour and bicarbonate of soda/baking soda into a mixing
bowl, and set aside.

In a small saucepan place the Guinness and butter, and heat over low
heat, until the butter has melted. Remove from heat and sift the cocoa
powder into the pan, add the sugar and whisk until all the lumps have
dissolved. Pour this mixture into a mixing bowl and set aside to cool.

In another bowl, beat the egg with the sour cream and vanilla bean
paste and then add this to the cooled cocoa mixture.

Gradually add the sifted dry ingredients, using a balloon whisk to mix
everything into a smooth, runny batter.

Divide the mixture between the muffin cases, then bake in the
preheated oven for 35–38 minutes, until well risen and a skewer inserted
into the cakes comes out clean. Transfer the cupcakes to a wire rack to
cool completely.

Prepare the Basic Cream Cheese Icing following the instructions on
page 21.

Spoon the cream cheese icing into the piping/pastry bag and pipe
icing onto each cupcake. Alternatively, spread the icing onto each cake
using a palette knife or metal spatula.

To decorate, carefully press chocolate shavings around the outside
of each cake. If you prefer to scatter them on the top of the cake, this
also looks fantastic.

Delicious coconut and rum sponge hides a tangy pineapple core. Finished with a coconut rum buttercream, these cupcakes are a tropical delight.

pina colada cupcake

YOU CAN'T GO WRONG WITH A COCKTAIL CUPCAKE, WELL THAT'S WHAT WE THINK AT LOLA'S! CLOSE YOUR EYES AND IMAGINE YOU'RE IN BARBADOS!

3 eggs
175 g/³/₄ cup caster/superfine sugar
115 ml/¹/₂ cup vegetable oil
65 ml/¹/₄ cup coconut cream or milk
175 g self-raising flour/1¹/₃ cups cake flour mixed with 2 teaspoons baking powder, sifted
40 g/¹/₂ cup desiccated/dried unsweetened shredded coconut

TO DRIZZLE
60 ml/¹/₄ cup coconut rum

BUTTERCREAM
200 g/1³/₄ sticks butter
350 g/3 cups icing/confectioners' sugar
2–3 tablespoons coconut rum
30 g/¹/₃ cup desiccated/dried unsweetened shredded coconut

Preheat the oven to 180°C (350°F) Gas 4.

Place the eggs and sugar into the bowl of a stand mixer fitted with a whisk attachment (or use a hand-held electric whisk), and beat the mixture at medium to high speed for 1–2 minutes, until light and fluffy.

If using a stand mixer, switch to the paddle attachment. Combine the oil and coconut cream or milk, then slowly add to the egg mixture, and mix just until combined. With the mixer set to low speed, add the sifted flour and desiccated/dried unsweetened shredded coconut, and beat until fully incorporated.

Using an ice cream scoop, divide the mixture between the muffin cases, filling to almost two-thirds full. Bake in the preheated oven for 20–25 minutes, until well risen and a skewer inserted into the cakes comes out clean. Transfer to a wire rack and, whilst the cupcakes are still warm, drizzle with some of the coconut rum. Allow to cool completely.

To make the buttercream, place the butter into the bowl of a stand mixer fitted with a paddle attachment (or use a hand-held electric whisk), and beat until smooth and soft. Sift in half of the icing/confectioners' sugar and mix at low speed, until fully incorporated. Add the second half of the sugar, then beat, slowly, until fully incorporated. Add the rum, a tablespoon at a time, mixing at medium speed, until the buttercream is light and fluffy. If the buttercream is too stiff, add a little more rum. Finally stir in the coconut, and set aside.

PINEAPPLE CORE

220 g/8 oz. canned pineapple in juice (either chunks or rings)
3 tablespoons coconut rum

TO DECORATE

toasted coconut flakes

muffin pan lined with 12 muffin cases

piping/pastry bag fitted with a large star nozzle/tip

MAKES 12

For the pineapple core, place the canned pineapple into the bowl of a blender with the rum and blend to a smooth purée. Set aside.

To assemble the cupcakes, use a sharp knife or apple corer to remove a small section from the centre of each cooled cupcake. Using a teaspoon (or disposable piping/pastry bag), fill the holes almost to the top with the pineapple purée.

Spoon the buttercream into the piping/pastry bag fitted with the large star nozzle/tip, and pipe stars of buttercream onto the top of each cupcake. Alternatively, spread the buttercream onto each cupcake using a palette knife or metal spatula.

Decorate the cupcakes with toasted coconut flakes. It is easiest to take small handfuls of the coconut flakes and press them into the buttercream icing to help them stick.

(You can also make mini versions of these cupcakes, as shown. The mixture will make about 36 mini cupcakes, and you will need a mini muffin pan lined with mini muffin cases. Bake them for 10–15 minutes, or until a skewer inserted into the cakes comes out clean.)

champagne cupcake

THE DELICATE AROMA OF CHAMPAGNE INFUSES THIS CUPCAKE AND GIVES A LIGHT TEXTURE TO THE SPONGE. SPOIL SOMEONE SPECIAL IN YOUR LIFE WITH THIS TREAT!

170 g/1 1/4 cups plain/
   all-purpose flour
2 teaspoons baking powder
160 g/1 1/2 sticks butter
160 g/3/4 cup plus 1
   tablespoon caster/
   superfine sugar
3 eggs
3 tablespoons Champagne
   (or other sparkling wine)

BUTTERCREAM
150 g/1 1/4 sticks butter
350 g/3 cups icing/
   confectioners' sugar
3–4 tablespoons Champagne
   (or other sparkling wine)

TO DECORATE
edible sugar pearls

muffin pan lined with
   12 muffin cases

piping/pastry bag fitted with
   a large star nozzle/tip

MAKES 12

Preheat the oven to 180°C (350°F) Gas 4.

Sift the flour and baking powder into a mixing bowl, and set aside.

Place the butter and sugar into the bowl of a stand mixer fitted with a paddle attachment (or use a hand-held electric whisk) and beat the mixture at medium to high speed for 1–2 minutes, until light and fluffy. Occasionally stop to scrape down the sides of the bowl with a rubber spatula, to make sure that all the butter and sugar is incorporated.

Combine the eggs and Champagne in a bowl and, with the mixer at low speed, add to the butter and sugar, mixing until fully combined.

Slowly add the sifted dry ingredients, and mix at low speed until combined. Scrape down the sides of the bowl with a rubber spatula, and briefly beat at high speed until the mixture is smooth. Do not over-mix.

Using an ice cream scoop, divide the mixture between the muffin cases, filling to almost two-thirds full. Bake in the preheated oven for 20–25 minutes, until well risen and a skewer inserted into the cakes comes out clean. Transfer the cupcakes to a wire rack to cool completely.

To make the buttercream, place the butter into the bowl of a stand mixer fitted with a paddle attachment (or use a hand-held electric whisk) and beat until soft and fluffy. Sift in half of the icing/confectioners' sugar and mix at low speed, until fully incorporated. Add the second half of the sugar, then beat, slowly, until fully incorporated. Add the Champagne slowly, mixing at medium speed, until the buttercream is light and fluffy.

Spoon the buttercream into the piping/pastry bag and pipe buttercream onto the top of each cupcake in a swirl or flower design. Alternatively, spread the buttercream onto each cake with a palette knife or metal spatula. Decorate the cupcakes with edible sugar pearls.

AFTER DARK

CHOCOLATE CHILLI CUPCAKE

CHOCOLATE MACADAMIA CUPCAKE

DARK CHOCOLATE TRUFFLE CUPCAKE

CHOCOLATE MINT CUPCAKE

BLACK BOTTOM CUPCAKE

chocolate chilli cupcake

IN THIS GROWN-UP TREAT, OUR BLACK BOTTOM BASE ACTS AS A CARRIER FOR A
DECADENT SPICY GANACHE. A COOLING CREAM CHEESE FILING IS CONCEALED INSIDE.

100 g/¾ cup plain/
  all-purpose flour
65 g/⅔ cup unsweetened
  cocoa powder
1 teaspoon baking powder
3 eggs
250 g/1 cup caster/superfine
  sugar
2 tablespoons full-fat/whole
  milk
175 g/1½ sticks butter, melted

GANACHE
300 ml/1¼ cups double/heavy
  cream
225 g/8 oz. plain/semisweet
  chocolate (up to 50% cocoa
  solids)
a pinch of ground cinnamon
½ teaspoon cayenne pepper
  or chilli/chili powder

CREAM CHEESE CORE
150 g/5½ oz. full-fat cream
  cheese
50 g/2 oz. dark/bittersweet
  chocolate (up to 70% cocoa
  solids), melted
25 g/1 oz. milk chocolate,
  melted

TO DECORATE
12 small red chillies/chilies

muffin pan lined with
  12 muffin cases

piping/pastry bag fitted with
  a large star nozzle/tip

MAKES 12

Preheat the oven to 180°C (350°F) Gas 4.

Sift the flour, cocoa powder and baking powder into a mixing bowl, and set aside.

Place the eggs and sugar into the bowl of a stand mixer fitted with a whisk attachment (or use a hand-held electric whisk), and beat the mixture at medium to high speed for 1–2 minutes, until light and fluffy.

If using a stand mixer, switch to the paddle attachment. Add the sifted dry ingredients to the batter, along with the milk, mixing at low speed. Add the melted butter and beat until blended. Do not over-mix.

Using an ice cream scoop, divide the mixture between the muffin cases, filling to almost two-thirds full. Bake in the preheated oven for 20–25 minutes, until well risen and a skewer inserted into the cakes comes out clean. Transfer to a wire rack to cool completely.

To make the ganache, place the double/heavy cream in a small saucepan and heat until almost at boiling point. Place the chopped chocolate, ground cinnamon and cayenne pepper or chilli/chili powder in a heatproof bowl. Pour the hot cream over the chopped chocolate and spices, and stir to combine. The mixture will be smooth and glossy. Allow to cool before placing in the refrigerator to set.

For the cream cheese core, simply place the cream cheese into a mixing bowl and beat with a wooden spoon, until soft. Pour in the melted chocolates and mix until fully blended.

Use a sharp knife or apple corer to remove a small section from the centre of each cupcake. Using a teaspoon (or disposable piping/pastry bag fitted with a small round nozzle/tip), fill the holes almost to the top with the cream cheese filling.

Remove the ganache from the refrigerator at least 15 minutes before you are ready to decorate. Spoon the ganache into the piping/pastry bag and pipe a star onto the top of each cupcake. Alternatively, spread the buttercream onto each cupcake using a palette knife or metal spatula.

Top each swirl with a red chilli/chili; it is up to you if you choose to eat this. You have been warned!

chocolate macadamia cupcake

THE BUTTERY MACADAMIA NUT LENDS ITSELF SO WELL TO THIS TRULY DECADENT CUPCAKE. A DARK CHOCOLATE SPONGE HIDES A CANDIED MACADAMIA CARAMEL CENTRE AND IS FINISHED WITH A RICH DARK CHOCOLATE GANACHE AND CANDIED WHOLE MACADAMIA NUTS. THIS ONE IS A BIG FAVOURITE WITH THE LOLA'S TEAM.

175 g self-raising flour/1 1/3 cups cake flour mixed with 2 teaspoons baking powder
50 g/generous 1/3 cup unsweetened cocoa powder
4 eggs
240 g/1 1/4 cups caster/granulated sugar
175 ml/3/4 cup sunflower oil
90 ml/3/4 cup full-fat/whole milk

CANDIED NUTS
100 g/1/2 cup caster/superfine sugar
100 g/1 cup macadamia nuts

FILLING
100 g/1/3 cup store-bought caramel

Preheat the oven to 180°C (350°F) Gas 4.

Start by making the candied nuts. Place the sugar in a saucepan and heat over medium heat until the sugar has melted and starts to caramelize. Do not stir the sugar; just swirl the pan so that all the granules are incorporated. Keep an eye on the sugar as it can burn very quickly. Once the sugar is a medium-brown colour, quickly tip the macadamia nuts into the caramel and swirl to coat. Pour the mixture onto the prepared baking sheet and allow to cool. Be careful as the sugar is very hot.

For the cake batter, sift the flour and cocoa powder into a bowl, and set aside.

Place the eggs and sugar into the bowl of a stand mixer fitted with a whisk attachment (or use a hand-held electric whisk), and beat the mixture at medium to high speed for 1–2 minutes, until light and fluffy.

If using a stand mixer, switch to the paddle attachment. Combine the oil and milk, slowly add to the egg mixture and mix until just combined. Gradually add the sifted dry ingredients to the batter, mixing at low speed until all the dry ingredients have been incorporated. Scrape down the sides of the bowl, and beat at high speed until the mixture is smooth. Do not over-mix.

Using an ice cream scoop, divide the mixture between the muffin

GANACHE

200 ml/²/₃ cup double/heavy cream

100 g/¹/₂ cup chopped dark/bittersweet chocolate (up to 40% cocoa solids)

baking sheet lined with baking parchment

muffin pan lined with 12 muffin cases

piping/pastry bag fitted with a large star nozzle/tip

MAKES 12

cases, filling to almost two-thirds full. Bake in the preheated oven for 20–25 minutes, or until risen and a skewer inserted into the centre of the cakes comes out clean. Transfer to a wire rack to cool completely.

To make the ganache, place the double/heavy cream in a small saucepan and heat until almost at boiling point. Place the chopped chocolate in a heatproof bowl. Pour the hot cream over the chopped chocolate and stir to combine. The mixture will be smooth and glossy. Allow to cool before placing in the refrigerator to set.

For the filling, blitz one-quarter of the candied nuts in a food processor, until fine. Mix into the caramel. Use a sharp knife or apple corer to remove a small section from the centre of each cupcake. Using a teaspoon (or disposable piping/pastry bag), fill the holes almost to the top with the macadamia caramel.

Remove the ganache from the refrigerator at least 15 minutes before you are ready to decorate. Spoon the ganache into the piping/pastry bag and pipe a swirl onto the top of each cupcake. Alternatively, spread the ganache on each cake using a palette knife or metal spatula. Decorate the cakes with the remaining candied macadamia nuts.

(To make mini versions of these cupcakes you will need a mini muffin pan lined with mini muffin cases. Bake for 10–15 minutes, or until a skewer inserted into the cake comes out clean. The mixture will make about 36.)

dark chocolate truffle cupcake

FOR THOSE OF YOU WHO ARE GLUTEN-INTOLERANT, THIS IS A GREAT RECIPE TO MASTER. THIS FLOUR-LESS CUPCAKE IS MOIST AND FUDGEY, AND WOULD MAKE A GLAMOROUS DESSERT SERVED WITH CRÈME FRAÎCHE AND FRESH BERRIES. WE LIKE TO SOAK OUR CAKE IN ORANGE LIQUEUR – THIS IS OPTIONAL BUT IT DOES ADD A RATHER DECADENT EDGE.

4 eggs
125 g/²⁄₃ cup caster/
    granulated sugar
170 g/1¹⁄₂ sticks butter,
    melted
120 g/4 oz. dark/
    bittersweet chocolate
    (up to 50% cocoa solids)
    melted
1 tablespoon unsweetened
    cocoa powder, sifted
65 ml/¹⁄₄ cup Grand Marnier
    (optional)

GANACHE
300 ml/1¹⁄₄ cups double/
    heavy cream
225 g/8 oz. chopped dark/
    bittersweet chocolate
    (up to 50% cocoa solids)

Preheat the oven to 180°C (350°F) Gas 4.

Start by making the ganache. Place the double/heavy cream in a small saucepan and heat until almost at boiling point. Place the chopped chocolate in a heatproof bowl. Pour the hot cream over the chopped chocolate and stir to combine. The mixture will be smooth and glossy. Allow to cool, then chill in the refrigerator until needed.

To make the cake batter, place the eggs and sugar into the bowl of a stand mixer fitted with a whisk attachment (or use a hand-held electric whisk), and beat the mixture at medium to high speed for about 3 minutes, until light and fluffy.

If using a stand mixer, switch to the paddle attachment. Add the melted butter and chocolate, and beat at medium speed, until fully combined. Sift in the cocoa powder and combine slowly, until the mixture is smooth.

Using an ice cream scoop, divide the mixture between the muffin cases, filling to almost two-thirds full. Bake in the preheated oven for 20–25 minutes, until well risen and a skewer inserted into the cakes comes out clean. Do not open the oven door during the cooking time or the cakes will collapse!

TO DECORATE
dark chocolate truffles
   (we use cocoa-dusted
   truffles)
edible gold leaf (books
   of 5 sheets are available
   online or from large
   supermarkets)

muffin pan lined with
   12 muffin cases

piping/pastry bag fitted with
   a large star nozzle/tip

MAKES 12

Transfer to a wire rack and, while still warm, drizzle a teaspoonful of the Grand Marnier over each cupcake, if using. Allow to cool completely on the wire rack.

Remove the ganache from the refrigerator 15 minutes before you are ready to decorate.

Spoon the ganache into the piping/pastry bag and pipe a swirl onto each cupcake. Alternatively, spread the ganache onto each cupcake using a palette knife or metal spatula.

To decorate, take a chocolate truffle and lightly dampen the top with some water on a paintbrush. With a dry paintbrush, carefully lift some of the gold leaf off its paper and drape over the dampened area so that it adheres to the truffle. Place in the centre of the swirl and repeat with the remaining truffles and cakes.

With so few other ingredients involved,
it is essential that you purchase good-quality
chocolate and cocoa powder when making
these decadent flourless cupcakes.

chocolate mint cupcake

THIS CUPCAKE REMINDS US OF CHILDHOOD SUMMERS AND MINT CHOCOLATE ICE CREAM. THIS CUPCAKE VERSION WILL NOT DRIBBLE DOWN YOUR ARM!

50 g/½ cup unsweetened cocoa powder

175 g self-raising flour/ 1⅓ cups cake flour mixed with 2 teaspoons baking powder

4 eggs

240 g/1¼ cups caster/ granulated sugar

90 ml/⅓ cup full-fat/whole milk

1 teaspoon peppermint extract

175 ml/¾ cup sunflower oil

75 g/½ cup plain/semisweet chocolate chips

BUTTERCREAM

150 g/1¼ sticks butter

¾ teaspoon peppermint extract

300 g/2½ cups icing/ confectioners' sugar

2–3 tablespoons full-fat/ whole milk

mint green food colouring paste

Preheat the oven to 180°C (350°F) Gas 4.

Sift the cocoa powder and flour into a bowl, and set aside.

Place the eggs and sugar into the bowl of a stand mixer fitted with a whisk attachment (or use a hand-held electric whisk), and beat the mixture at medium to high speed for 1–2 minutes, until light and fluffy.

If using a stand mixer, switch to the paddle attachment. Combine the milk, peppermint extract and oil, and slowly add to the egg mixture, mixing just until combined. Slowly add the sifted dry ingredients, mixing at low speed, until all the dry ingredients have been incorporated. Scrape down the sides of the bowl with a rubber spatula, and beat at high speed until the mixture is smooth. Do not over-mix.

Fold in the chocolate chips, until evenly distributed.

Using an ice cream scoop, divide the mixture between the muffin cases, filling to almost two-thirds full. Bake in the preheated oven for 20–25 minutes, until well risen and a skewer inserted into the cake comes out clean. Transfer to a wire rack to cool completely.

To make the buttercream, place the butter into the bowl of a stand mixer fitted with a paddle attachment (or use a hand-held electric whisk), and beat until soft and fluffy. Add the mint extract and mix again, until combined. Sift in half of the icing/confectioners' sugar and mix at low speed, until incorporated. Add the second half of the sugar, then beat, slowly, until incorporated. Add the milk, a tablespoonful at a time, mixing at medium speed, until the buttercream is light and fluffy. If the buttercream is too stiff, add a little more milk. Using the tip of a sharp knife take a small amount of the food colouring paste and add it to the

TO DECORATE
**dark/bittersweet chocolate
truffles**
**chopped dark/bittersweet
chocolate**

*muffin pan lined with
12 muffin cases*

*piping/pastry bag fitted with
a large star nozzle/tip*

MAKES 12

buttercream. Blend until the colour is your desired shade, but do not over-mix. Spoon the buttercream into the piping/pastry bag, and pipe a swirl of buttercream onto each cupcake. Alternatively, spread the buttercream onto each cake using a palette knife or metal spatula.

Decorate each cupcake with a chocolate truffle and some chopped dark/bittersweet chocolate.

black bottom cupcake

THIS CUPCAKE COMBINES CHOCOLATE SPONGE WITH A CREAMY WHITE CHOCOLATE CHEESECAKE FILLING TO MAKE SOMETHING QUITE SPECIAL. THE CHEESECAKE LAYER HELPS TO KEEP THIS CAKE MOIST AND DELICIOUSLY DIFFERENT. WE HAVE ADDED A BLUEBERRY COMPOTE TOPPING TO REALLY TIE ALL THE FLAVOURS TOGETHER.

100 g/ $^3/_4$ cup plain/ all-purpose flour
65 g/ $^2/_3$ cup unsweetened cocoa powder
1 teaspoon baking powder
3 eggs
250 g/1 $^1/_4$ cups caster/ granulated sugar
2 tablespoons full-fat/whole milk
175 g/1 $^1/_2$ sticks butter, melted

CHEESECAKE CORE
100 g/3 $^1/_2$ oz. full-fat cream cheese
50 g/ $^1/_4$ cup caster/granulated sugar
1 teaspoon vanilla bean paste
1 egg
75 g/2 $^1/_2$ oz. white chocolate, melted

Preheat the oven to 180°C (350°F) Gas 4.

Start by making the cheesecake core. Beat together the cream cheese and sugar in a small bowl with a wooden spoon. Add the vanilla bean paste and egg, and mix, then pour in the melted white chocolate, and stir to combine. Set aside until needed.

For the cupcakes, sift the flour, cocoa powder and baking powder into a mixing bowl and set aside.

Place the eggs and sugar into the bowl of a stand mixer fitted with a whisk attachment (or use a hand-held electric whisk), and beat the mixture at medium to high speed for 1–2 minutes, until light and fluffy.

If using a stand mixer, switch to the paddle attachment. Add the sifted dry ingredients to the batter along with the milk, mixing at low speed to combine. Add the melted butter and beat to blend. Do not over mix.

Spoon 2 teaspoons of cheesecake filling into the bottom of each muffin case, then, divide the cake mixture between the muffin cases, filling to almost two-thirds full. Bake in the preheated oven for 20–25 minutes, until well risen and a skewer inserted into the cakes comes out clean. Transfer to a wire rack to cool completely.

For the compote, place all of the ingredients into a small saucepan and gently heat to allow the berries to soften and their juices to run. Simmer for 2–3 minutes, until the compote is slightly thickened and the

BLUEBERRY COMPOTE
150 g/1 cup blueberries
2 tablespoons water
2 tablespoons caster/
 granulated sugar
1/2 tablespoon freshly
 squeezed lemon juice

CREAM CHEESE ICING
60 g/1/2 stick butter
1 teaspoon vanilla bean paste
200 g/1 1/2 cups icing/
 confectioners' sugar
400 g/14 oz. full-fat cream
 cheese

*muffin pan lined with
 12 muffin cases*

*piping/pastry bag fitted with
 a large star nozzle/tip*

MAKES 12

consistency of a soft jam/jelly. Set aside to cool.

To make the cream cheese icing, place the butter into the bowl of a stand mixer fitted with a paddle attachment (or use a hand-held electric whisk), and beat until smooth and soft. Add the vanilla bean paste and sift in the icing/confectioners' sugar. Add the cream cheese and beat at medium to high speed for about 30 seconds, until smooth and glossy. Do not over-mix.

Spoon the cream cheese icing into the piping/pastry bag and pipe a swirl onto each cupcake. Alternatively, spread the icing onto each cupcake using a palette knife or metal spatula.

Top each cupcake with a teaspoonful of the blueberry compote.

To achieve the two-tone look of our black bottom cupcake, you can either place the cheesecake filling in the bottom of each muffin case, or pipe into the middle of the batter as a hidden surprise. The choice is yours!

index

acknowledgements

With thanks to all the hard-working bakers, decorators and the rest of the Lola's team in the bakery and stores who all contribute to making Lola's a fun and exciting place to work. Special thanks to Julia Head, who developed the cupcake recipes, and Robert Budwig. Thank you to Peter Cassidy, Bridget Sargeson and Jenny Iggleden for bringing the recipes to life with stunning photography, and thanks to Tracy Davy for the gorgeous illustrations. Thanks to Adrian Sharman for all his help with the inspiration and design of the Lola's rebranding and for the fabulous sketches. Finally, thank you to Cindy Richards, Julia Charles, Leslie Harrington, Sonya Nathoo, Kate Eddison, Alice Sambrook and all at Ryland, Peters & Small for producing such a beautiful book.